Walt
Whitman

Milton Meltzer

Walt Whitman

A Biography

Twenty-First Century Books
Brookfield, Connecticut

Also by Milton Meltzer

Carl Sandburg: A Biography

Langston Hughes: A Biography

Dorothea Lange: A Photographer's Life

Ten Queens: Portraits of Women of Power

Ten Kings and the Worlds They Ruled

Witches and Witch-Hunts: A History of Persecution

They Came in Chains: The Story of the Slave Ships

*Weapons and Warfare: From the
Stone Age to the Space Age*

There Comes a Time: The Struggle for Civil Rights

Lincoln in His Own Words

Frederick Douglass in His Own Words

Library of Congress Cataloging-in-Publication Data

Meltzer, Milton, 1915–
Walt Whitman : a biography / by Milton Meltzer.
p. cm.
Includes bibliographical references (p.) and index.
Summary: A biography of the nineteenth-century poet, which presents
his life in the context of his times, and includes samples of his writing.
ISBN 0-7613-2272-8 (lib. bdg.)
1. Whitman, Walt, 1819-1892—Juvenile literature. 2. Poets, American—
19th century—Biography—Juvenile literature. [1. Whitman, Walt,
1819–1892. 2. Poets, American. 3. American poetry.] I. Title.
PS3232 .M35 2001   811'.3—dc21 [B]
2001027798

Published by Twenty-First Century Books
A Division of The Millbrook Press, Inc.
2 Old New Milford Road
Brookfield, Connecticut 06804
www.millbrookpress.com

Contents

I Hear America Singing

I hear America singing, the varied carols I hear,
Those of mechanics, each one singing his
as it should be blithe and strong,
The carpenter singing his as
he measures his plank or beam,
The mason singing his as he makes ready
for work, or leaves off work,
The boatman singing what belongs to him
in his boat, the deckhand
singing on the steamboat deck,
The shoemaker singing as he sits on his bench,
the hatter singing as he stands,
The wood-cutter's song, the ploughboy's on his way
in the morning, or at noon intermission
or at sundown,
The delicious singing of the mother, or of the
young wife at work, or of the girl sewing
or washing,
Each singing what belongs to him
or her and to none else,
The day what belongs to the day—at night
the party of young fellows, robust, friendly,
Singing with open mouths their
strong and melodious songs.

Foreword

Walt Whitman wrote one book of poetry in his life—*Leaves of Grass*. He published nine editions, each time adding lines, subtracting lines, changing words, always trying to make it better.

"A poet's work," one poet said, "is to find words for the sense of life he learns more and more surely to recognize in himself." Some people need to express themselves by building a fence, or a computer. Some need to dance, or paint pictures. Some to make money, or plant a garden. Others need to collect trophies, or collect facts. Whatever they do, it is their way of expressing their sense of life.

Poets, too, find pleasure in doing such things. They are not different from ourselves, except in one way. That difference is in their use of words, the choosing of them, the placing of them on the page in such a way as to voice their sense of life.

Whitman? A poet, yes, but by the standards of his society not a success. He had no real career as most people think of it. At one time or another he was a carpenter, teacher, printer, journalist, shopkeeper, real estate speculator, nurse, clerk.

Perhaps it was the very ordinariness of his occupations that gave him the materials out of which he constructed his masterpiece. In *Leaves of Grass* he was the first to reveal the glory of everyday things. He captured the emotions and imaginations of Americans, the people he loved.

"I give the sign of democracy," he says in a poem. "All the men ever born are also my brothers, and the women my sisters and lovers, I am large, I contain multitudes.

Stranger, if you passing meet me and desire to speak to me, why should you not speak to me?

And why should I not speak to you?"

"I think of art," he declared, "as something to serve the people—the mass; when it fails to do that it is false to its promises." And then he added, "If *Leaves* is not for the average man, it is for nobody."

Chapter 1

Form'd From This Soil, This Air

ALT WHITMAN WAS BORN ON MAY 31, 1819. His birthplace was West Hills, near Huntington, New York, a village on fish-shaped Long Island, which stretches 118 miles east from New York City along the edge of the Atlantic Ocean. It was only thirty years since the creation of the world's first democratic republic, the United States of America. The country's population was just under ten million.

Walt was the second son of Walter and Louisa Whitman. The Whitmans were among the earliest English settlers in America. The family of Walt's mother, the Van Velsors, was descended from early Dutch settlers.

For generations both sides of the family had been farmers. The house Walt was born in was built by his father, who did carpentry now and then. It was a plain two-storied wooden house with sloping roof, its sides covered by weather-worn shingles. The entrance was sheltered by a little square porch, shadowed by flowering shrubs. The house stood amidst hundreds of family-owned acres. Nearby was the family's burial ground.

Walt rarely felt warmly toward his father, a man hard to live with—harsh, moody, sometimes a heavy drinker. Yet he was a thoughtful man. He liked to read widely, and books were always at hand. He fathered nine children and named three of his sons after presidents he admired: George Washington, Thomas Jefferson, and Andrew Jackson.

In his children he planted seeds of a radical patriotism. Take nothing for granted, ask questions, think for yourself! Farmers, laborers, craftsmen—the people who do the work

Whitman's birthplace in West Hills,
Long Island, New York

of the world, were the best, he taught them. Don't look to the rich and the powerful for anything. They are the enemy.

Mr. Whitman had been a friend of Tom Paine, the Englishman who came to America as the revolution was birthing. His pamphlet, *Common Sense*, helped bring about the Revolutionary War by making Americans realize that independence was their true goal and that a democracy was vastly better than a monarchy. Paine's writings were cherished in the Whitman household, and so was the *Free Enquirer*, the paper edited by the radical thinkers Frances Wright and Robert Dale Owen.

When Walt was ten, his parents took him to hear the radical Quaker preacher, Elias Hicks. Although too young to follow the lecture closely, Walt never forgot the transforming power of Hicks's oratory. The Quaker's appeal to the "inner light" of religious spiritualism and the "outer light" of revolutionary enlightenment would become central to the poet's thought. Walt saw Jefferson as the democrat in politics and Hicks as the democrat in religion.

He took pride in his ancestry for its role in the American Revolution. In George Washington's earliest combat with the British—the Battle of Brooklyn on August 27, 1776—one of Walt's granduncles, Nehemiah Whitman, fought and died. Walt never forgot that date, reliving the day in his mind and re-creating it in a poem called "The Centenarian's Story." General Washington himself was Walt's hero. He placed him at the heart of his poem "The Sleepers."

He treasured the traditional agrarian ways of his ancestors, even as they disappeared. Some of his poems re-create his rural background. You can see it in *Leaves* where he wrote these lines:

> To hear the birds once more,
> To ramble about the house and barns and over the fields
>   once more,
> And through the orchard and along the old lanes once
>   more.

Or again:

Whitman's manuscript revision of <u>Song of Myself</u>

My tongue, every atom of my blood, form'd from this soil,
this air,
Born here of parents born here from parents the same, and
their parents the same.

Yet his nostalgia had little to do with reality. For Walt's family, like so many others, would be forced to face great change—economic and cultural.

Chapter 2

The Best Part of Any Man

I N 1819, THE YEAR OF WALT'S BIRTH, the young nation was just becoming aware of two powerful forces that threatened to shake America to its foundations. Remember that the United States was a group of states only loosely joined together under the Constitution. Regional and economic differences placed obstacles to true unity.

One of these powerful forces was the issue of slavery. In 1800 a million slaves labored in all parts of the country.

Several of Walt's own family had been slaveholders. On his mother's side, the Van Velsors, one ancestor had owned sixteen slaves. "We all kept slaves on Long Island," Walt recalled, and up to the early part of his century. One of his constant companions when a youth was a liberated West Hills slave called Mose.

Gradually, the number of free blacks grew. Some of the Northern states prohibited slavery. Some slaves freed themselves by running away, some were given freedom by their masters, some bought their freedom.

A long and stormy debate over whether slavery should be extended into the territories and new states of the Union was quieted for a time by passage of the Missouri Compromise in 1820. Missouri was admitted as a slave state, and Maine as a free state, thus making a sectional balance of twelve states each. By law, slavery was now to be prohibited "forever" in any new U.S. territory north of Missouri.

To old Thomas Jefferson, news of the bitterness and fiery passion of the debate came "like a firebell in the night," tolling the "knell of the Union."

He was right. The Compromise did not end the bitter quarrels. The slavery issue would erupt throughout Walt's childhood and youth and become a vital part of his work as a young journalist.

The other powerful force was economic. A great depression began in 1819, the first of several that have periodically racked the country's capitalist economic system ever since. America's agricultural economy was being overtaken by a new market economy. It would develop giant corporations, create multimillionaires, and widen the gulf between the rich at the top and the masses of poor people at the bottom.

Most families until now had produced on their farms whatever they needed. They were self-sufficient. They did not buy in commercial marketplaces. They lived off the land, and usually in homes passed down from generation to generation. Hadn't the Whitmans lived on their Long Island acres since 1660? No wonder Walt's poems praised farm life. Yet the reality changed abruptly for them. When Walt was nearly four, his father was forced to leave West Hills and move the family to Brooklyn, which was just beginning to grow from a village to a city. Young Walt kept going back to Long Island, spending summers with his grandmothers on their farms, and rambling over the fields and beaches.

Life would not be easy for the Whitmans. Of Walt's seven siblings, two went mad and one was retarded. The family was never able to settle down. They moved almost every year as Walt's father picked up work building or renovating small houses. He speculated on being able to sell them, but often lost both house and investment. Much later Walt wrote about these hard times in his prose work, *Specimen Days*. His father's money troubles helped him to understand how business worked and the effect of politics on it.

Whitman's parents, Walt Sr. and Louisa

All around him young Walt saw victims of that first economic depression. His parents spoke often and bitterly of the "idle rich" and praised the men and women who defended working people against oppression. It made Walt sensitive to the popular arts—stories, music, plays—that voiced their needs and aspirations.

About Walt's mother, Louisa, we don't know very much. In his writings he always praised her highly, calling her "the ideal woman, practical, spiritual, of all of earth, love, to me the best." Late in life he said, "The best part of any man is his mother." She was a good storyteller, he claimed, with a gift for impersonation. She endured much—constant financial trouble, her husband's moodiness and drinking, severe problems with some of her many children.

Walt learned from his mother what good parenting meant. Although he never married, he acted like a father to many young people he encountered in his adult years.

Chapter 3

Bred in Brooklyn

WALT SPENT TWENTY-EIGHT YEARS OF his life in Brooklyn. "I was bred in Brooklyn," he said. There he knew the joys and suffered the disappointments that would prepare him for the poetry he would write. When the Whitmans moved in, Brooklyn was only a village. Within a few decades it would boast a population of 200,000, making it the nation's fourth largest city. (It would not become part of New York City until 1898.)

A winter scene in the Brooklyn of Walt's boyhood

Manhattan, as seen across the bay from Brooklyn

America in the 1820s was still almost completely without the conveniences (now we say the necessities) we have long taken for granted. You got water from street pumps and carried it home in a wooden bucket. Garbage littered the streets. No central heating. Each room in your house had to be warmed by its own fireplace. You moved about on foot, on horseback, or in carriages. And so, too, from city to city, for the transcontinental railroad wouldn't come until 1869. And of course no electric lights, no telephone or telegraph, no cars or planes, no radio, no television, no movies, no computers.

Yet the world was at Walt's doorstep. On the Brooklyn Ferry he often crossed the sweeping bay of New York into Manhattan. The waterfront was crowded with ships delivering cargo, and the flood of immigrants on their way to a better life they dreamed they would enjoy in the New World. Many would build the new railroads, dig the canals, put up the housing. Others found work in the factories rising out of the Industrial Revolution.

At the age of six, Walt started school. Brooklyn had only one public school then, a place for "charity scholars," sneered the elite who sent their children to private schools. Still, he was lucky, for a great many Brooklyn children never went to school. Soon a second school was opened, but both schools had only two teachers for some two hundred students. The older white children were taught in the basement, the youngest on the first floor, and the black children segregated on the top floor.

Teaching was dictatorial in these huge classes. Do what I say, and don't ask questions! Memorize, memorize! There were Bible readings and moral preachments, plus reading and writing, arithmetic and spelling and geography. A few grades higher, the courses added were grammar, geometry, history, and some of the sciences. Disobey the teacher and you were beaten. Later, in his first venture into print, Walt condemned school flogging.

One teacher described Walt as "a big, good-natured lad, clumsy and slovenly in appearance." Later, when that teacher heard that Walt was now a famous poet, he said it proved "We need never be discouraged over anyone."

Walt wasn't a great scholar. He didn't stay long in school, for at eleven he was forced to leave because his family needed whatever wages the boy could earn.

Going to work at this young age was common. By the early 1800s half the nation's textile workers were under ten and were working twelve or more hours a day. Most people didn't think this was a bad thing. They believed in the essential goodness of work, and had a strong fear of idleness. Children from four to ten years old operated machinery in iron mills and got twelve to twenty-five cents for a day's labor. Children who stayed home on the farm—they were the majority—had many hard chores. At twelve a boy could be plowing a field, splitting rails, building fences, and sickling at harvest time.

And so Walt's long job history began. Two lawyers took him on as office boy. One of the partners tutored him, and broadened his reading by giving him membership in a circulating library. He enjoyed tales of frontier life by James Fenimore Cooper, the exotic stories of *The Arabian Nights*, and the novels and poetry of Sir Walter Scott.

Soon he moved on to a clerkship in a doctor's office. And then, at twelve, came an opening to the world of newspaper publishing. The editor of the weekly *Long Island Patriot* took him on as an apprentice. That year he learned how to set type by hand.

The newspapers of that time—the "penny press"—were mostly one-man operations, though sometimes with apprentices to help. The publisher was both printer and reporter. He wrote the pieces, set the type, ran the press, handled the business side, maybe kept his press busy by turning out books, too.

That experience of a single person doing the whole job would influence Walt when it came time for him to publish the many editions of *Leaves*.

A year later, at thirteen, Walt began working for a Brooklyn printer. An outbreak of the dreaded disease cholera, killed thirty-five people in Brooklyn and led the Whitmans to move back to the countryside near West Hills. Walt, however, stayed on, joining the weekly *Long Island Star* as a compositor. After nearly three years at that job, he switched to setting type for a printer in Manhattan.

A print shop typical of those in which young Walt worked

On both the *Patriot* and the *Star* a few of Walt's first efforts at writing got into print, without his name signed. One of his editors who had lived through the Revolutionary War enjoyed telling Walt how such great men as Washington and Jefferson and Franklin looked and acted. The newspapers openly served the interests of one political party or another. Walt learned how powerful the printed word could be in advancing political goals. There were two major political parties at the time. Workers supported the Democrats, and manufacturers the Whigs.

Walt's hunger for reading never let up. His newspaper work required him to read even more to gather information for reporting. He found nothing was alien to him. Everything fed his inner life. Especially all that dealt with the rights, the opportunities, and most of all the potentialities of ordinary people. He hoped that step by step they would advance on the long journey of humanity toward personal freedom and full self-development.

The notebooks he kept from the early 1840s tell us what he read and absorbed. He was after facts, concrete realities he observed that would one day enrich his poetry. Scribbled in the notebooks are both prose and poetry.

Chapter 4

Never Mind What People Think

T THE BEGINNING OF HIS POEM "Song of Myself" Whitman tells us

> I loafe and invite my soul;
> I lean and loafe at my ease observing a spear of
> summer grass . . .

Was he lazy? Many people thought so. They noticed how relaxed he was. He never gave the impression that he was driving toward some goal, nearby or distant. He moved slowly, taking his own time, resisting a boss's orders to hurry up, get it done now. The biographer Philip Callow said:

> Whitman's innate resistance to the will of others was part of his sly, undeclared disobedience, a refusal to go along with the world. If his mother said worriedly, "What will people think?" her strange son with his contradictory moods, his changeable restless nature, would answer quietly, "Never mind what they think."

Perhaps it was this desire to take it easy that left him free to soak up, slowly but steadily, his impressions of the world around him. Yet despite the seeming idleness, here was a man who would write many thousands of pages— reams of newspaper articles and editorials, letters, stories, and the immense *Leaves of Grass*.

In the early 1800s, newspapers began springing up everywhere. By 1830 there were thirty-six daily papers. Twenty years later there were over 250. Journalists rarely stayed put. They moved from paper to paper, just as Walt did. By the time he was fifteen, he looked more grownup than youngster, tall, and inclined to heaviness, and no longer dependent on his parents.

30

In 1833 Walt saw a happening he would never forget. President Andrew Jackson, just beginning his second term, was making a "Grand Triumphal Tour" of the Northeast. Mounted on a horse, he led a parade up Broadway to City Hall Park, with 100,000 people roaring a welcome from the housetops and streets. They adored Jackson because they felt he carried on the radical message of Jefferson's Declaration of Independence. They applauded his open contempt for selfish business leaders, the "money power." They

Andrew Jackson, president-elect, on his way to Washington

ignored his autocratic ways, his constant demand that everything must go his way. The majority of voters had re-elected Jackson as a great populist leader who spoke for them. The sight of grizzled Old Hickory, waving his beaver hat at the applauding crowds, thrilled the young Whitman.

Jackson's nature, a bit like Whitman's, was contradictory. He believed in both liberty and power. How do you balance them? That tension was expressed in the nation's politics. In a democracy, which comes first, the rights of the individual or the rights of society? Which should it be, state sovereignty or national power?

In the 1830s New York went through some terrible times. Those who led a movement for Congress to outlaw slavery became the targets of mob violence. Egged on by pro-slavery politicians and newspapers, people broke up Abolition meetings, stoned the movement's leaders, wrecked or burned their homes, and destroyed their presses. In New York in 1834 anti-black rioters attacked black churches, and tried to lynch two leaders of the Abolition organization. Three days of near-madness were ended only when troops were called in.

In December 1835 a great fire of unknown origin swept through the city, burning down 674 buildings at a loss of many millions of dollars. Thousands of newspaper workers were put out of work by the ravages of the flames and remained idle for a long time. The failure of a wheat crop led to what was called the Flour Riot of 1837. Merchants were accused of hoarding wheat and flour in their warehouses in order to hike their prices. The rich were wallowing in luxury while the poor had no bread, claimed street speakers. Rioters broke into food stores and destroyed barrels of flour and sacks of wheat, wrecked warehouses, invaded offices, and might have killed food merchants had not soldiers been sent in to capture the ringleaders.

To much of this Walt was witness. Although he opposed slavery, the passionate devotion of the Abolitionists to their cause and the violence of the resistance against them deeply disturbed him. Couldn't slavery be ended peacefully? Must the conflict between the two sides end in civil war, tearing apart his beloved nation?

While many journalists quit New York to seek jobs elsewhere, Walt tried to hang on. But in May 1836 it was starve—or go back home to Long Island where his family could feed him. His father expected him to take over farm chores; Walt would have none of that. Instead, he got a job teaching school in East Norwich, not far from his maternal grandfather.

Here he was, only seventeen, with but a few years of schooling himself, in charge of a one-room schoolhouse. It wasn't hard to find work teaching. Teachers moved around a lot. Within some five years Walt taught at eight different schools, among them Norwich, Hempstead, Babylon, Southold, Long Swamp, Smithtown. School terms were short. In one place Walt was paid $72.50 plus board for five months' teaching. The pupils ranged from first graders to some his own age.

Unlike most teachers of his time, Walt didn't use physical punishment. He tried to change bad behavior by talking to the child. He didn't want to act like a drill sergeant, bossing everyone around. He preferred that students learn to think for themselves. The task was to help children understand the subject, not just memorize facts about it. He knew children are born curious. They ask questions about everything they encounter as they grow. They have

The one-room schoolhouse at Southold, Long Island,
New York, where Walt taught

a natural hunger for knowledge. And books don't have all the answers; you can learn a lot from life itself. He wished all schools would teach music and poetry and provide playgrounds.

How good a teacher was he? Some liked him a lot. Others said no, he seemed to forget where he was now and then, and spent too much time at his own writing. He was trying his hand at short stories and poems. They were so routine and sentimental it is hard to believe the same man could create *Leaves of Grass*. At the heart of some stories was the conflict between a son and a father who treated him badly. Maybe they were autobiographical. When between teaching jobs, Walt would return home, and the conflict with his father

34

would pick up again. Nevertheless, Walt liked being with his family, now enlarged to eight children. Young though he was, he acted as though he were their father, as well as their companion. He wrote once that "Though a bachelor, I have several boys and girls that I consider my own."

While teaching in Smithtown, Walt joined a local debating club. The records of the debates give us a glimpse into his thinking at that time. He opposed slavery, encouraged foreign immigration to the United States, advocated abolition of capital punishment, and argued that the early colonists had done wrong in mistreating the Native Americans.

Briefly, in 1838, while between teaching jobs, Walt started his own newspaper. He bought a second-hand printing press and in Huntington launched a weekly called the *Long Islander*. He covered local happenings, provided weather and harvest reports, and wrote a column offering parental advice. He was not above playing up sensational stories to draw readers. On horseback, he delivered his paper to subscribers on a thirty-mile circuit. But there were too few readers, and besides, he disliked the business side of the venture. He sold the paper within a year.

A few months later Walt found work as a typesetter on the *Long Island Democrat*. He also wrote for the sheet. He published his first poem here, in 1838. Some of his other writings rode the current passion for reform, urging readers not to use tobacco, coffee, or tea—this when almost all American men chewed tobacco and smoked cigars. After a year at the paper, he picked up teaching again, earning the typically small sums for the short terms.

Later, as he returned to newspaper work, Walt often wrote about education. In one of his poems, "By Blue Ontario's Shore," there are such lines as these; asked of readers.

Are you faithful to things? do you teach what the land and
    sea, the bodies of men, womanhood, amativeness,
    heroic angers, teach?
Have you sped through fleeting customs, popularities?
Can you hold your hand against all seductions, follies,
    whirls, fierce contentions? are you very strong? are you
    really of the whole People?. . .
Do you hold the like love for those hardening to maturity?
    for the last-born? little and big? and for the errant?
What is this you bring my America?

Whitman, says the poet Ron Padgett, "was as tough as
he was tender." And the Nobel laureate poet from Chile,
Pablo Neruda, tells us: "What really counts is that Whitman
was not afraid to teach—which means to learn at the hands
of life and undertake the responsibility of passing on the
lesson."

Chapter 5

Creating Your Own Way

URING WALT'S TEACHING YEARS THE nation suffered another depression, worse than the one of 1819. It began with the Panic of 1837. There was little control over speculation. Fraud and mismanagement were widespread. Paper money fell in value everywhere. Banks collapsed. The Southern planters plunged deeply into debt. Prices of essential foods soared out of reach for the poor.

The terrible effects were felt by all classes. Farmers and factory workers suffered the most. Right into the early 1840s about a third of the working people were jobless for long periods of time.

The ravages of the depression were blamed by the Whigs on the policies of Andrew Jackson, who left office early in 1837. The America he turned over to his successor, President Martin Van Buren, slid rapidly into the pit. The depression dragged on for six miserable years, hitting bottom in 1842.

Walt saw the depression as the result of a war between capital and democracy. Businessmen driven by their hunger for personal profit were trying to stamp out the energies of young America. Walt and the other young Democrats looked back in history to Jefferson and Paine, to the Declaration of Independence as a living document that launched "the political regeneration of the world."

These were years when Walt developed ideas not only about good teaching but about the craft of writing, too. While the depression of 1837–1842 did untold harm to a vast number of people, it had a creative effect upon American literature. Though Walt drifted from job to job, barely keeping his head above water, the experience would enrich his writing. Herman Melville, born the same year as Walt, was forced to go to sea when his family's business failed. Out of that life came the great novel *Moby Dick*. Ralph Waldo Emerson found the time of the depression to be his most creative period. In those same years Henry David Thoreau, whose father's pencil factory was hurt, turned away from trade to live the solitary life, out of which he created *Walden*.

Walt was not the only one to develop fresh ideas about better ways to teach children. Up in Massachusetts, the reformer Horace Mann was urging educators to quit using harsh authoritarian methods in favor of more creative ways to stimulate young minds. Bronson Alcott (the father of Louisa May, who wrote *Little Women*) also tried out progressive practices at his new school in Boston.

In Walt's approach to writing poetry you can see the application of his teaching experience. Just as he believed the learner should be taught to rely on himself, so he believed the poet should create his own way of writing poetry. Not to be imitative, not to copy the forms, the rhythms, of others—especially the English poets who dominated literature on this side of the Atlantic. And not to limit himself to the themes other poets had treated, no matter how worthy they might be.

At the same time, he wanted others to do as he would do. That paradox is clear when he says, "I teach straying from me, yet who can stray from me?" And "He most honors my style who learns under it to stray from the teacher." One of his poems he titles "To a Pupil."

Young people, excited by reading a novel or a poem they love, often dream that one day they, too, will write what all the world will read. "I would compose a wonderful and ponderous book," Walt said in one of his newspaper pieces. "Therein should be treated on, the nature and peculiarities of men, the diversity of their characters, the means of improving their state, and the proper mode of governing nations. And who shall say that it might not be a very pretty book?"

He wrote this in 1840, when a slam-bang presidential election was getting under way. For the first time, Walt became politically active. He made stump speeches and debated for the Democrat, Martin Van Buren, even though the Democrats were against congressional interference with slavery. The Whig candidate was General William Henry Harrison. Both parties ignored the issues and campaigned on personalities. On a scale never tried before, each party charged the other with evasion, lies, abuse, misrepresentation, irrelevancies. Walt himself was threatened with violence because he had called a Whig editor a "liar and blackguard." One wing of the Abolition movement had formed a Liberty Party, but its candidate, James G. Birney, got only 7,000 votes. For the first time in twenty years the Democrats lost, and Harrison took over the White House

Whitman had turned twenty-one. What did he look like now? One of his former students later recalled him as a ruddy-faced young man, wearing a black frock coat, a vest, and black trousers, Walt would have many pictures taken of himself down through the years. In the first one, made in the early 1840s, he looks very much the gentleman, in fashionable clothes and sporting a cane, with a superior smile.

Walt's poetry in *Leaves* would sing the praises of Americans, the workers and farmers who were the base of Jackson's democracy. But when he was teaching, he wrote the unkindest words about the Long Islanders around him. "Clowns and country bumpkins," he called them in a letter

Walt in his twenties

to a friend, "flatheads, and coarse brown-faced girls, dirty, ill-favored young brats, with squalling throats, and crude manners, and bog-trotters, with all the disgusting conceit, of ignorance and vulgarity . . . the grossest, most low-minded of the human race."

Why was he so angry? Why did he seem to hate these villagers? One biographer, David S. Reynolds, holds that in documentation he discovered it appears that while teaching school, Walt may have had sexual contact with a male student in whose home he was boarding. The story goes that when he was denounced from the pulpit by the minister, a mob chased Walt down, tarred and feathered him, and rode him out of town on a rail.

No court or church records refer to this. The sources are items in the local press and oral history passed on through the generations. People who knew Walt observed that girls did not attract him. Reynolds says that "At the very least, Whitman's feelings for young men were particularly ardent expressions of the kind of same-sex passion that was common among both men and women in nineteenth-century America. Such ardor was in fact widely accepted in the street culture of Brooklyn and New York, but in a Puritan-based rural town . . . it would have been frowned upon, whether or not it involved sexual contact."

Whether the story is true or not, Walt never taught school again. He returned to Manhattan, finding work in 1841 as a printer for a weekly paper, the *New World*.

Chapter 6

Delights
of the City

THERE WAS HARDLY ANY KIND OF publication Walt did not work or write for in the 1840s. Why did he change jobs so often? Sometimes because his employers disliked his politics. Or because his laid-back attitude angered the boss. Or because another paper offered him a better deal—more pay, and freedom to write on whatever he chose.

"Whatever" included writing about the delights of the city. New York was now the nation's biggest city, but its

Busy Broadway, in Walt's early days as a journalist

300,000 inhabitants had not yet pushed past Twenty-third Street. Beyond that point were the rural areas where wealthy people built summer homes. Broadway's cobblestones clattered with horse-drawn traffic from the Battery to where the wide road thinned out to country lane four miles away. The green before City Hall was *the* park, and the Astor House was *the* hotel, boasting 300 rooms at a dollar a day.

For boys, New York above Twenty-third Street was almost like the wilderness. They roamed at will through farmlands and woods, playing by the rivers and ponds, running after the volunteer firefighters. One amusement was to chase the hogs scavenging on the garbage-littered streets, to try to catch them with a lasso made from old clothesline.

In the eyes of the Massachusetts writer Lydia Maria Child, who came to edit an abolitionist paper, New York was "this great Babylon," a scene of "magnificence and mud, finery and filth, diamonds and dirt, bullion and brass." Its contrasts struck her: "Wealth dozes on damask couches while poverty camps on the dirty pavement. There, amid the splendor of Broadway, sits the blind Negro beggar, with horny hand and tattered garments, while opposite to him stands the stately mansion of the slaveholder."

Irish and German immigrants were pouring into New York. They were not warmly welcomed, only grudgingly accepted as badly needed labor for the new industrial economy. They had to have places to live, and housing was built for them as well as for new businesses. Day by day New York kept moving uptown, the "old families" of the Dutch and the English building elegant new houses while the newcomers crowded into tenements.

Not everyone who entered the port of New York stayed on. Thousands took steamers at Buffalo for Cleveland or Detroit and then, by foot or by horse, they pushed farther into the heart of the vast continent. From Cincinnati and Saint Louis, too, they went, leapfrogging across the country in an unending stream of humanity, following their dreams of happiness.

To entertain them on such long trips there was plenty to read. Most of it was trash—stories like *Nellie the Ragpicker's Daughter*—but other and better books were also written—by Byron, Tennyson, Dickens, and Scott from Britain, and by the American poets Longfellow, Lowell, Whittier, Holmes, Bryant. Emerson had begun writing his essays, Cooper his novels, Melville his South Sea romances, Hawthorne his sketches.

Walt, too, had his try at a novel, calling it *Franklin Evans*. Published in 1842, as part of a "Books for the People" series, it proved to be his most popular work, selling about 20,000 copies during his lifetime. It came out in pamphlet form, priced at twelve and a half cents.

Walt created the story to advance the cause of temperance reform. He was against laws banning the use of liquor. He believed instead that reform was best gained through persuasion. His story gave many examples of the unhappy effects of drinking, with Evans in the end learning to take a total-abstinence pledge. In old age Walt referred to his novel as "damned rot of the worst sort."

A revolution was taking place in journalism as Walt quit teaching and returned to New York. The big and stodgy four-page sheets that had bored readers since Ben Franklin's time with their endless sermons and speeches were giving way to the penny papers. The new cylinder press and other technical advances had made daily newspapers possible, and cheap enough at a penny to reach everyone, everywhere. For the first time there was real news, fresh news, news gathered by that rising professional, the reporter. The editors

PARK BENJAMIN, EDITOR.

FRANKLIN EVANS,

OR

THE INEBRIATE.

A TALE OF THE TIMES.

BY A POPULAR AMERICAN AUTHOR.

"Oh, thou invisible spirit of wine, if thou hast no name to be known by, let us call thee—Devil!"   SHAKSPERE.

NEW-YORK:
J. WINCHESTER, 30 ANN-STREET.

1842.

PRICE 12½ CENTS.

J. WINCHESTER, PRINTER,
30 Ann-street, New-York.

Title page of Franklin Evans

offered scandals, miracles, and horrors. They invented the personal interview and concentrated on the sensational.

The press influenced the whole country, giving America the news, although news selected and often distorted by the owners' peculiar prejudices and politics. In 1841, a young man from New Hampshire, Horace Greeley, entered the field with his *New York Tribune*, another penny paper—but with a difference. His aim was "to advance the interests of the People, and to promote their Moral, Social and Political well-being."

During these years Walt changed his living quarters almost as often as his job. He moved from one lodging house to another, gaining some peace and quiet only in 1845 when he settled near his family in Brooklyn.

No one could accuse Walt of living in a narrow rut. In his writing he tried nearly everything, sticking to no one style or theme. Most writers found their niche, and especially if it paid off, stayed with it. But not Walt. David Reynolds, after a close study of some forty-odd imaginative works by Walt in the years before *Leaves*, described the great variety of poems and tales as pieces about death or haunted minds; sensational and adventurous; visionary, picturing angelic visitations; reformist; patriotic or nationalistic; political, moral, and biblical.

Walt was well aware of what was popular, and as a newspaper editor he printed many sensational stories of violent crimes. At the same time that he provided this stuff for his readers, he attacked villainous lawyers, bankers, landlords, and other upperclass people. One of his favorite crusades was opposition to the death penalty. In one of his stories a murderer escapes being caught and, feeling great remorse for his crime, heroically nurses the victims of a cholera epidemic. Walt ends the tale pointing out that executing this man would have made life no better, while his repentant social work saved the lives of others.

One of Walt's early poems portrayed an author who died alone and friendless. The man was McDonald Clarke, a street drifter called the Mad Poet of Broadway. Clarke often used rhyme, but varied his lines in length and mixed slang with polished diction. Sometimes playful, sometimes erotic, but more often desolate, the poems made a strong impression on Walt.

Walt's own poetry would show the influence of Clarke's work. He picked up, too, on the recent readiness of writers to treat more imaginatively the sacred texts of the Bible, placing himself within fictional biblical scenes. Like many popular writers, he was sentimental about the Founding Fathers of the Revolution, finding consolation for the ugly quarrels of his day in veneration of those golden years.

Chapter 7

A Glorious Opportunity

WALT'S RETURN TO JOURNALISM CAME at an exciting moment. Young newsmen had been electrified by the powerful example set by William Leggett. Writing for the *New York Evening Post* in the 1830s, Leggett's fiery language and biting wit urged his readers to recover the passion of the Revolution and to move it forward.

Among the young especially there was an optimistic faith in their own power to make the new nation fulfill the promise of the ideals that had inspired the Declaration of Independence. Americans had founded a democracy, but much more was needed to perfect it. And Walt was one who believed that nothing less than perfection would do.

What is man born for, Emerson asked, "but to be a Reformer, a Remaker of what man had made, a renouncer-of-lies, a restorer of truth and good?"

A tide of reform flooded the country in the early 1840s. Men and women took up the battle against privilege and injustice. They attacked the new factory system for employing women and children for cruelly long shifts at pitiful wages, the landlords for the slums spreading in the cities, the southern planters for the sin of slavery. They attacked governments seeking to settle their differences by war, men for treating women like chattels. They took up the cause of prison reform and of decent treatment for the handicapped and the insane. They fought for free schools, for equality of taxation, for labor's right to organize, and for cheap land.

Leggett's contempt for the old leaders of the Democratic Party led thousands of young New Yorkers to challenge their dominance. His success proved the press could spread new ideas to an immense number of sympathizers. Journalism, he said, gives us a "glorious opportunity" to advance the cause of mankind.

Leggett showed that the press, wisely used, could launch a cultural as well as a political revolution. His writing was evidence that you could offer new ideas to people who had not dared to think before. "It calls into exercise minds that before rusted unused."

When Walt reentered journalism it was no longer a routine trade. Leggett and Greeley had given it glamour, especially if you were young and out to make a difference in the world. Walt would often speak of "the glorious Leggett," shaping a new generation called "Young America."

He continued to be active in politics. Speaking in 1841 at a Democratic rally of 15,000 people, he said, "We are battling for great principles—for mighty and glorious truths." He was a guiding spirit of his party, but the slavery issue, the Mexican War, states' rights, labor strife, and capitalist domination threatened to dissolve not only the Union but democracy itself.

In the writing Walt did for several papers, he often followed the political line of the *Democratic Review*, a new paper. Many young people worried that America was forgetting its revolutionary heritage. Wasn't the Panic of 1837, and the long depression it set off, evidence that the Old Guard politicians had failed to meet the nation's needs? They had acted selfishly, concerned only for profit-making. Many young Americans like Walt had pitched in to the 1840 election because they felt the future of the republic was at stake.

The thinking of this new generation was much like that of the same generation in Europe. There, students and young radicals were joining political groups seeking to get rid of monarchies, struggling to free the Old World of its ancient habits and prejudices.

In America, Emerson had sounded a challenge to youth in a famous speech at Harvard College. Speaking to students in 1837 he called for books meaningful to the new generation of Americans: "Each age, it is found, must write its own books. The books of an older period will not fit this." Later Walt reported the lectures Emerson gave in New York.

The confidence that youth could do anything arose in part from an awareness of what a great number of them there were. In 1840 the median age of Americans was just under eighteen. Over 12 million of the country's 17 million people—or roughly three out of four—were under thirty.

The 1840s was a turbulent decade that saw fierce combat, in both politics and on the battlefield. John L. O'Sullivan, when he launched the *Democratic Review*, had said America's "manifest destiny" was to spread democracy across the North American continent. Expansion was all very well if there was nothing in the way of it. But soon Americans were forced to think about war as the price of expansion. Settlers in the Texas territory were for annexation even if it meant war with Mexico. Settlers in California talked openly of tearing that rich province away from Mexico.

The issue of expansion became thoroughly entangled with the issue of slavery. Both North and South were concerned with the national balance of power. The North feared that taking over the vast Texas territory would add a new slave domain and thus tilt the scales against the free states.

There was intense debate in Congress and among the people over the issue. In the end, President Polk began a war with Mexico in 1846. In 1848 the defeated Mexicans signed a peace treaty, conceding to the United States 500,000 square miles, about one-third of Mexico's land. It was more than the combined area of France, Spain, and Italy. The United States had grown enormously through its aggression.

Now the basic question was: How would the new territories be organized? Would they come into the Union as free states or slave states?

A minority of Americans opposed the war. As American troops were advancing into Mexico, Henry David Thoreau was jailed in Concord. Years before, he had refused to pay his poll tax to support a government that sanctioned slavery and now was fighting a war to extend it. Thoreau believed that a man of conscience had a right to resist his government when it did wrong. His essay on civil disobedience argued that the law is not to be respected merely because it is the law, but only because it is right and just.

Walt, however, like O'Sullivan, the *Review*'s editor, believed in the war. And in the *Brooklyn Eagle* he wrote: "Yes, Mexico must be thoroughly chastised!" He called for America to take over California, too, saying it would cause an "increase of human happiness and liberty."

The Young Americans had a kind of mystical faith that victory over Mexico would signify, in Walt's words, the coming of a "holy millennium of liberty." Herman Melville, too, exulted that "the political millennium had come." Both saw Manifest Destiny as the expression of their generation's dream of world unity. It was the American Revolution happening all over again, on a world scale now.

At this same time, an unknown young man from Illinois, upon entering Congress in 1847 spoke out against the Mexican War, charging President Polk with distorting the truth. This view lost Abraham Lincoln supporters back home. They made this his first and last term in Congress. The prairie lawyer sank back into obscurity—for a time.

Lincoln was not alone in protesting the war. Another Congressman, Joshua Giddings of Ohio, told the House:

> This war is waged against an unoffending people, without just or adequate cause, for the purposes of conquest; with the design to extend slavery; in violation of the Constitution, against the dictates of justice, of humanity, the sentiments of the age in which we live, and the precepts of the religion we profess. I will lend it no aid, no support whatever. I will not bathe my hands in the blood of the people of Mexico. . . .

Whitman was not blinded for long by the nationalist fervor. As the decade wore on, with increasingly ferocious political quarrels, he and other writers hoped that a great literature would bring Americans together, and prevent the bloody chaos of sectional and class conflict: "Let us be Americans—not Northerners or Southerners—but simply Americans."

It was a brief experience in the South that modified his views. Not long after leaving the *Eagle*, Walt was asked to work for a New Orleans paper, the *Crescent*. In 1848 he went south to take on the job. His fourteen-year-old brother, Jeff, went along as an apprentice, paid five dollars a week. They went by rail, stagecoach, and steamboat, a torturously slow journey. Although they stayed only three months, the experience broadened Walt's outlook on American life. The city's population was richly mixed—African American, Native American, French, Hispanic, Anglo-American. The ethnic and cultural variety was fascinating. But he was working for a paper that ran ads for slave sales, and walking the streets he saw slaves being auctioned off. After observing the worshippers in the cathedral, young Jeff wrote home to his parents that "everyone would go and dip their fingers in the holy water and then go home and whip their slaves."

It was a first-hand experience that made Walt feel in his bones what extending slavery in America would mean.

When Walt learned that a new Free Soil political party was being formed, he wanted to be part of it. He quit the *Crescent* and the South and returned to New York. The Whitman brothers left New Orleans in late May, heading home. On the way they stopped to see St. Louis, Chicago, Milwaukee, Cleveland, Buffalo, and Albany. Now Walt had learned something of the cities, rivers, prairies, and mountains of almost every part of the then United States. The experience would gradually be reflected in *Leaves of Grass*.

Chapter 8

Making Every Word Draw Blood

**A**S SOON AS HE GOT BACK IN TOWN, A newspaper announced that Whitman had returned, "large as life, but quite as vain, and more radical than ever." He was elected as a delegate to the Free Soil convention in Buffalo. It nominated Martin Van Buren as its presidential candidate, on a platform of "free soil, free speech, free labor, and free men."

Backed by Brooklyn Free Soilers, Walt promptly launched a two-penny paper, the *Brooklyn Freeman*. "Under all circumstances," he wrote, he would "oppose the addition

The offices of Whitman's paper,
the Brooklyn Freeman, on Fulton Street

to the Union, in the future, of a single inch of *slave land*, whether in the form of state or territory."

But just after his first issue came out, a fire destroyed several blocks of the neighborhood, including his newspaper office.

Meanwhile, Walt bought a lot and built a house, and here he opened a bookstore. Now his mind turned more to poetry and oratory as perhaps a better way than journalism to reach people and shape their views.

With the decade of the 1850s about to begin, the political pot was coming to a boil. The new territories gained in the Mexican War were seeking admission to the Union. Should they come in as free or slave states? Congress met in December 1849 with both Democrats and Whigs divided into warring factions over slavery, and with the minority of Free Soilers holding the balance of power.

The country, after remaining the same size for a quarter of a century, had nearly doubled in territory—by treaty and by conquest—in the single term of President Polk. Repeated threats of disunion, voiced often, alarmed the great body of citizens. Couldn't some kind of give-and-take settle the issue and clamp down the mounting sectional antagonism?

As the debate began, Senator Henry Clay of Kentucky proposed a compromise in the hope of settling sectional grievances. Three issues stood out: slavery in the territories, slavery and the slave trade in the District of Columbia, and the fugitive slaves who were finding shelter in Northern states.

After a long and intense debate, Clay's "amicable arrangement" was embodied in laws known as the Compromise of 1850. It provided for the admission of California as a free state; the other territories carved from Mexico would decide the slavery question for themselves. A new and harsher fugitive slave law would force the North to return runaways to their owners, and the interstate slave trading based in the District of Columbia would be suppressed.

As he followed the debate, Walt became more and more disgusted by how often Northern congressmen yielded to the Southerners, acting like dough shaped in their hands. He published a poem called "Song for Certain Congressmen" in the *New York Evening Post* in which he condemned "dough-faced politicians." How could such senators as Daniel Webster seek to save the Union by approving the buying and selling of human beings?

With the passage of the Compromise the ideals of the Revolution were betrayed. In another poem, "Blood-Money," printed in Greeley's paper, Walt accused Webster and others of acting like Judas selling the body of Christ. They, too, for personal gain, were selling out black men and women. In still other poems of this time of crisis Walt began to go beyond conventional verse, using unrhymed lines varying in length:

> Arise, young North!
> Our elder blood flows in the veins of cowards—
>
> . . . .
> Fight on, band braver than warriors,
> Faithful and few as Spartans;
>
> But fear not most the angriest, loudest, malice—
> Fear most the still and forked fang
> That starts from the grass at your feet.

In the early 1850s Walt wrote freelance articles for the press and did odd jobs building houses in Brooklyn. It gave him time to work on his poems, feeling his way to a free verse style. In the election of 1852 the Democrats and Whigs both accepted the Compromise of 1850, while the Free Soilers opposed the Compromise and slavery itself. Franklin Pierce, the Democrat, won, while the Free Soil man got only a small number of votes.

Disappointed, Walt decided that he himself had to do his best to rekindle the radical fire for freedom that still must burn in the hearts of Americans. In his notebook he jotted down plans for roving through the whole country delivering a series of lectures he called "lessons." A note pictures himself at an abolition meeting, "punctual to the hour, ascends the platform, silent, rapid, stern, almost fierce—and delivers an oration of liberty—upbraiding, full of invective—with enthusiasm."

Whether he ever did this, and how often, we don't know. He goes on to support the right of the slave to revolt, and his determination to assist him, "whether he be black or whether he be white, whether he be an Irish fugitive or an Italian or German or Carolina fugitive, whether he come over sea or over land, if he comes to me he gets what I can do for him."

Now, in his defiance of the Fugitive Slave Law, Walt sounds like Thoreau. And later in the poem in *Leaves of Grass* called "Song of Myself," he offers the "lesson"—

> The runaway slave came to my house and stopt outside,
> I heard his motions crackling the twigs of the woodpile,
> Through the swung half-door of the kitchen I saw him
>   limpsy and weak,
> And went where he sat on a log and led him in and assured
>   him,
> And brought water and filled a tub for his sweated body and
>   bruis'd feet,
> And gave him a room that enter'd from my own, and gave
>   him some coarse clean clothes,
> And remember perfectly well his revolving eyes and his
>   awkwardness,

And remember putting plasters on the galls of his neck and
    ankles;
He staid with me a week before he was recuperated and
    pass'd north,
I had him sit next me at table, my firelock lean'd in the
    corner.

It was this spirit of revolt that flared again when the fugitive slave Anthony Burns was arrested in Boston in May 1854 and ordered by a federal court to be returned to his Virginia master. The news led to a mass attempt by citizens to protest Burns's arrest. They rushed to the courthouse where Burns was held and battered down the doors in an effort to free him. Constables and deputies fought them off and one man was killed. When Burns was sentenced to be returned to slavery, twenty-two military units were assembled in Boston to see that Burns did not escape, and a cannon was set up in front of the courthouse. Then, with Burns in their midst, the police and troops marched to the dockside through streets lined by a crowd of 50,000 persons hissing and crying "Shame!" At one point the populace tried to break through the guards and rescue Burns. Several people were injured. As the ship sailed for Virginia with Burns aboard, the crowd on the dock kneeled in prayer.

How could federal, state, and local authorities, in the very city where freedom was born, force a man back into slavery? That year, on the Fourth of July, the abolitionist editor William Lloyd Garrison publicly burned a copy of the Constitution as a symbol of the death of freedom.

Walt, too, demonstrated his protest in one of his earliest poems to be included in *Leaves*. "A Boston Ballad" he called it. What the American colonists went to war to *stop*, eighty years ago, we were now keeping up a war to *advance*. Was the America of today willing to sacrifice the principles of lib-

A Boston poster announcing the seizure of
Anthony Burns, a fugitive slave

erty for the pursuit of material wealth? "By God," he wrote, "I sometimes think this whole land is becoming one vast model plantation thinking itself well off because it has wherewithal to wear and no bother about its pork."

Walt had come to believe that agitation was the only way to save his democracy from political corruption. He was not alone in that, for many of the social reformers were whipping up a spirit of agitation in the hope of rousing the moral conscience of the nation. In his 1856 notebook Walt wrote: "Agitation is the test of the goodness and solidness of all politics and laws and institutions. If they cannot stand it, there is no genuine life in them, and shall die . . ." In such an age as this, he believed the poet "must make every word he speaks draw blood." In one of his poems he says, "I am he who walks the States with a barb'd tongue, questioning every one I meet."

In his poem "The Sleepers," Walt says, "I have been wronged . . . I am oppressed . . . I hate him that oppresses me/I will either destroy him or he shall release me." In his anger he lashed out against politicians, calling them lice, maggots, vermin. Fraud, lying, cheating by local, state, and federal government became so notorious in the 1850s it sickened Walt. He could never set it aside or close his eyes to it, though other poets might write only of roses and nightingales and lovely afternoons on Long Island beaches.

The reformer Thomas Low Nichols, reviewing that decade, wrote: "It is a matter of worldwide notoriety that during the past ten years whole legislatures have been bribed, that the state and national treasuries have been despoiled of millions, that members of Congress have sold their votes in open market to the highest bidder."

What troubled Walt as much as the corruption in government was the growing gap between rich and poor. While the cost of living for the poor shot up, the upper class grew fatter and fatter. Protest novels became popular, dramatizing scheming banks and lawyers getting wealthier while the poor starved. In "Song of Myself," Walt used a rural image to get across the charge that the rich prospered on the labor of the poor:

> Many sweating, ploughing, thrashing, and then the chaff
>   for payment receiving,
> A few idly owning, and they the wheat continually claiming.

Walt's disgust with the decay of the American system he shared with the radical socialists. Yet he didn't want to overthrow it and replace it, as they did. In the 1840s and 1850s a movement to create utopian communities swept in many reformers. Over twenty-five such movements sprang up in the North. Their aim was to get rid of the unfair capitalist system and replace it with cooperative communities where everyone shared both the work and living arrangements. (Brook Farm in Massachusetts was probably the best-known community.)

Walt leaned more to the individualists, people who believed in the right of every person to do as he pleases. They looked upon every man or woman as absolute sovereigns over their own lives—an almost inevitable tendency when you recognize how corrupt government authority had become. Emerson's celebration of Self Reliance permeated the reform movement, and Thoreau's *Walden*, published in 1854, strengthened it.

It was during the 1850s that Walt's individualism began to be reflected even in his choice of clothing. So too with

Portrait of Whitman made in 1854, used as the
frontispiece for the first edition of <u>Leaves of Grass</u>

many other men who decided to dress as they pleased, rather than as fashion dictated. While the rich looked super-elegant, Walt went in for plain, rough, loose-fitting clothing, crowned by a round felt hat.

Though a great agitator for reform, Walt was never a revolutionary. He shied away from any kind of extremism. He never wanted to rip up the Constitution and start all over again with something totally new. Change, yes, when needed and not destructive. Although sometimes he did use language that called for violent change. When he spoke of his hatred for the Fugitive Slave Law he said, "It is at all time to be defied in all parts of These States, South and North, by speech, by pen, and, if need be, by the bullet and the sword."

Chapter 9

I Thought I Had Something to Say

"B Y THE BULLET AND BY THE SWORD . . ." Those fierce threats could have been declaimed from the stage by Junius Brutus Booth, one of the powerful actors whose sensational performances Walt adored. Booth's "genius," Walt said, "was one of the grandest revelations of my life, a lesson of artistic expression."

Booth's intense acting of Richard III, Othello, Iago, Lear in Shakespeare's tragedies stirred Walt's emotional nature as nothing else did. So taken was he with performance that while walking the streets, strolling on the beaches, or crossing on the East River ferry, Walt would recite passages from the plays. "I spouted on the Broadway coaches," he told his friend Horace Traubel, "in the awful din of the street. In that seething mass—that noise, chaos, bedlam—what is one voice more or less: one single voice added, thrown in, joyously mingled in the amazing chorus?"

Playing a part became so habitual with Walt that a friend noted "he ceased to be conscious that he was doing it." And he would do it in his poetry. "His poetry was his grandest stage," says Reynolds, "the locus of his most creative performances." The "I" so often repeated in *Leaves of Grass* is everyone and everything Walt identified with— whether it be a fugitive slave or a clock: "I do not ask the wounded person how he feels. I myself become the wounded person."

Theater in Walt's time was inseparable from oratory. This was the golden age of speechifying. The masters of oratory—John C. Calhoun, Daniel Webster, Henry Ward Beecher, Wendell Phillips, Frederick Douglass—could count on American audiences for wild enthusiasm.

Junius Brutus Booth in costume

It was in the 1850s that Abraham Lincoln and Stephen Douglas were holding seven celebrated debates in Illinois, with the slavery issue at their heart, contesting for a seat in the U.S. Senate. Theirs was a more personal style of oratory, drawing from the great crowds a give-and-take. It encouraged Walt to give his poems an air of spontaneity, as though he were talking directly to the reader.

In the early 1800s a new medium for public speaking had been introduced—the lyceum. Lecturers traveled from town to town, seeking to satisfy the public hunger for knowledge and understanding. For a small admission fee you could find out what was going on in the arts, the sciences, religion, philosophy, literature. Emerson lectured, Thoreau lectured, and so did dozens of others.

As a youngster Walt wanted to be one of those up there on the lyceum platform, speaking his heart and mind to admiring crowds. "I thought I had something to say," he recalled later. "I was afraid I would get no chance to say it through books; so I was to lecture and get myself delivered that way."

He wrote out many lectures in the 1850s. His notebooks indicate he believed he could earn a living this way. Only one lecture of his has survived, delivered in 1851 before the Brooklyn Art Union. It reveals how strongly he felt a cash-on-the-barrel America needed art. Americans, he said, "view most things with an eye to pecuniary profit. . . . Matter of fact is everything, and the ideal nothing. He does a good work who calls to the feverish crowd that in the life we live upon this beautiful earth, there may, after all, be something vaster and better than dress, and the table, and business, and politics. . . .To the artist, I say, has been given the command to go forth unto all the world and preach the gospel of beauty. . . . It is a beautiful truth that all men contain something of the artist in them."

But art, he went on, "includes more than primal beauty." It embraces heroic human behavior as well. "I think of few heroic actions which cannot be traced to the artistical impulse. He who does great deeds does them from his sensitiveness to moral beauty. . . . Read how slaves have battled against their oppressors—how the bullets of tyrants have, since the first King ruled, never been able to put down the unquenchable thirst of man for his rights."

Walt liked reaching the ear of the people so directly. The desire would shape the oratorical style of his poems—their grand rolling lines with their rhythmic, repetitive speech patterns. Walt's poems often sound like spontaneous oratory, words spoken aloud. He tried out lines in his notebooks, scribbling down images, phrases, words as they came to him and later forming them into the complete poem. He tried them out on himself, speaking the lines aloud. That personal approach would appeal to readers, for they felt a man was talking directly to them, thinking with them, answering their questions, explaining mysteries. He often went to the Broadway Tabernacle, where famous orators spoke to huge crowds, and said he learned much from them. He liked orators with the common touch, the skill with everyday language that could reach even the humblest person.

Why would people in such great numbers turn out to hear someone make a speech? The reason is plain: It was entertainment. Recall that there were few other ways to be diverted from your work and your worries. Radio, television, movies were in the distant future. So were such sports as basketball and football that today draw vast crowds. With his sturdy ego it is no wonder Walt dreamed of being the center of mass attention.

Walt himself, it was said, had many of the elements that make a great speaker, but he could not project his voice to reach large audiences. That voice, however, could reach them on the printed page.

Music was as strong an influence on Walt as oratory. He often uses musical terms in his poetry, and even works in trumpets or cellos by name, as well as the titles of operas and symphonies. It was the human voice that stirred him most deeply. He believed music could unite and uplift a people afflicted by political corruption and in danger of breaking apart. What they shared, he said, was "their delight in music, the sure sympathy of manly tenderness and native elegance of soul."

New York offered both classical and popular music, the one for the upper class, the other for the working class. Soon, however, both of these levels became intermixed. In the mid-1880s the Hutchinson family singers with their antislavery songs and the minstrel groups with their plantation music became very popular. But so was Jenny Lind, the Swedish Nightingale, an operatic soprano whose concert tours of America, offering something for every level of listener, were a sensation.

In his poetry, Walt drew images from several cultural sources. Singing, instrumental music, and dancing, in all their forms, he would weave into his own poetic voice. He used a free-flowing style that expressed the common American experience, the ordinary lives of you and me and the family next door.

In this Walt was different from the writers whose fame long preceded his. Washington Irving, William Cullen Bryant, Henry Wadsworth Longfellow—they were the gentry. They belonged to that upper class or wished to identify themselves with it. They wrote elegant prose and poetry in forms approved by the best people. Theirs was a starched respectability.

Not so Walt's writing. Traditional? Conventional? Far from it. He was crafting a poetry that would break all bounds.

Chapter 10

I Celebrate Myself

HOW DO YOU WRITE A POEM? IS IT THE inspiration of the moment? Or does it lie in the mind for who knows how long, and then suddenly erupt on paper?

Scholars who have studied Whitman closely think that the poems in *Leaves of Grass* germinated for a long time before ripening. As we've seen, Walt began writing in his youth. But much of what he produced for newspapers and magazines—and his novel, too—was commonplace. His creative imagination had not been touched.

Then, gradually, his inner life struggled to the surface and began to speak. We know how widely he read, and his notebooks show he was responding to the power of poets. In his notebooks of the mid-1840s there is a mass of lyric prose, writing rhythmic even when not in verse. And poems too, often in response to events or things that delighted him or infuriated him. The poems, often unfinished, are early drafts of what would find their way into *Leaves of Grass*.

How does this happen, how does a genius emerge from the mind and heart of a busy man earning his way in the trade of journalism? Some say the poems are created by spiritual intuition. Others think Walt's genius was to absorb everything in his physical and spiritual environment, and then, under the pressure of experience, and with the skills he acquired, to create his poetry.

Certainly he was acutely conscious of what he was trying to accomplish. Again and again he notes his ideas of what a poet should be like, how he should compose, even what kind of success he should strive for. "Make it plain," he advised himself. "Lumber the writing with nothing—let it go as lightly as a bird flies in the air—or a fish swims in the sea." He wanted "a perfectly transparent, plateglassy style, artless, with no ornaments."

Walt published *Leaves of Grass* in 1855. He was 36 years old, the exact midpoint of his life. (He would die in 1892, at the age of 72.) Now, he thought, he was truly a poet. For the rest of his life he kept working on it, improving it—revising, adding, crafting his masterwork. *Leaves* would go through nine editions, the last appearing the year he died.

Edmund Wilson, the eminent literary critic, said that so many remarkable American books were "written to tell what a terrible place America is. I can think of only one great American book written to tell how somebody enjoyed America: Walt Whitman's *Leaves of Grass*."

Here are the opening lines of the long poem called "Song of Myself" that took up more than half of the first edition of *Leaves*. It conveys the poet's rapturous union with earth and spirit:

> I celebrate myself, and sing myself,
> And what I assume you shall assume,
> For every atom belonging to me as good belongs to you.
>
> I loafe and invite my soul,
> I lean and loafe at my ease observing a spear of summer
>   grass.
>
> My tongue, every atom of my blood, form'd from this soil,
>   this air,
> Born here of parents born here from parents the same, and
>   their parents the same,
> I, now thirty-seven years old in perfect health begin,
> Hoping to cease not till death.

How did Walt come to title his book *Leaves of Grass*? While reading a scientific work he had noticed "leaves" was the term broadly used to signify the green parts of all plants, including grass. Of course "leaves" also means the pages of a book. So his book, like green leaves, would spring up everywhere and nourish its readers.

He had his poem and his title. Now he had to get the book published. He wanted to reach literally everyone with his art and his beliefs. It would be hard for an unknown poet to find a publisher, for poetry rarely reaches broad audiences.

Well, he would publish the book himself. Rome's print shop in Brooklyn took on the job. It was close by the Whitman home (where Walt was living with his family) and he would walk to the printer every morning and sit by while the sheets of poetry came off the press. "I always superintended," he said, "and sometimes undertook part of the work myself, as I am a printer and can use the 'stick,' you know."

He took advantage of what technology made possible. *Leaves* was issued in varied formats, appealing to readers from all classes. He priced the editions from $2 to $1 to 75 cents.

When readers opened that first edition they found it didn't look like the typical book. No author's name was signed to the ninety-five-page volume, yet there on the title page was the picture of a strong bearded man, his collar open, with one hand in his pocket and the other on his hip. Who was he? If you read to page 29, in the poem later called "Song of Myself," the poet declared himself as "Walt Whitman, a kosmos, of Manhattan the son."

Walt's preface was printed in columns, like a newspaper page. And the twelve untitled poems that followed? They defied the rules of punctuation. Instead of commas, semicolons, and periods, Walt used ellipses. His lines of verse

LEAVES OF GRASS
IMPRINTS.

THAYER & ELDRIDGE,
Publishing House, 116 Washington St.

To the Public.—*In putting before you our new and superbly printed electrotype edition of America's first distinctive poetry, the "LEAVES OF GRASS," we offer the accompanying brochure as a circular to all persons disposed to commence the study of the Poems. We supply it gratuitously.*

☞ *The notices refer to the previous and partial issues of the Poems. See the 2d page of Imprints within. But all the pieces of previous issues are comprehended in our New Volume, with much additional matter.*

☞ *See last page for Publishers' advertisement.*

BOSTON,

June, 1860.

Just Published.
WALT WHITMAN'S
LEAVES OF GRASS.

☞ AN ELEGANT BOOK.

The publishers wish to call the attention of the reading world to ☞ the superior manner in which they have produced the "LEAVES OF GRASS." The typography will be found to vie in elegance with any thing ever issued from the American or English press. The paper is thick, white, and of superfine quality; the electrotyping from the Boston Stereotype Foundry; the printing by Rand, has been done with extreme care, with the best of ink; the binding is substantial and unique; the steel portrait, by Schoff, (from a painting by Charles Hine, of New York,) will enhance the reputation of that first-rate artist.

The work, as a whole, will be found to be an ornament to any book-shelf or table; and as such the publishers confidently claim for it a recognition as

One of the finest specimens of modern book making.

We wish it distinctly understood that the inferior style of print, typography, &c., spoken of in the notices in the foregoing circular, refer altogether to the previous, temporary and partial issues of the poems, and not at all to the superb edition we now present to the public.

The work comprises 456 pages, 12mo.

Price $1.25.

Copies will be mailed to any address in the United States, including California, postage paid, on receipt of the retail price.

THAYER & ELDRIDGE, Publishers,

114 & 116 Washington St., Boston.

Cover of a pamphlet Whitman issued
to promote Leaves of Grass

didn't appear in stanzas but flowed on without interruption. You could hardly tell where one poem ended and another began. Walt seemed to want you to read the book as one long poem. It was an organic form of free verse, with no concern for technical rules of style, or strict rhyme or meter.

The Young America movement Walt had been part of hoped for an American literature that would express "nativity, Americanness." But in its "purest, highest, broadest sense." Walt leaped over those limits. He would use the daily idioms and style, the living mode of expression. He wanted the distinctive tang of wild strawberry, of wild grape. His ear picked up and wove into his verse the spontaneous and vital idioms and slang expressions coined by the American masses.

Although many think of *Leaves* as Walt telling the world how wonderful America was, the contrary is true. He was responding to the signs he saw of the decay of the democratic tradition, its corruption, its possible death. He feared liberty was slipping away rapidly, and needed to be saved.

How different *Leaves* was from the poetry Americans grew up on! Longfellow was tightly bound to the tradition of the English poets. His work, like theirs, was the product of "culture and refinement." A poem like his "Song of Hiawatha"—its rhythm, its language—borrowed from the Europeans. What Walt wrote was remote from what the Harvard professor would bring into his literature classes. Nor did Walt find in Lowell, Whittier, or Poe much that would make him feel these were his brothers in art.

The book was quickly on sale in Brooklyn, New York, Boston, Philadelphia, and England. Walt saw that copies reached Longfellow, Whittier, and Emerson. Reviewers did not know quite how to take it. The *New York Tribune* said it would "awaken an interest in the lovers of literary curiosities." Another critic declared that "aside from America, there is no quarter of the universe where such a production could have had a genesis."

Within a few weeks, Emerson had read *Leaves* and on July 21 wrote Walt a glowing letter:

DEAR SIR—I am not blind to the worth of the wonderful gift of "LEAVES OF GRASS." I find it the most extraordinary piece of wit and wisdom that America has yet contributed. I am very happy in reading it, as great power makes us happy. It meets the demand I am always making of what seemed the sterile and stingy nature, as if too much handiwork, or too much lymph in the temperament, were making our western wits fat and mean.

I give you joy of your free and brave thought. I have great joy in it. I find incomparable things said incomparably well, as they must be. I find the courage of *treatment* which so delights us, and which large perception only can inspire.

I greet you at the beginning of a great career, which yet must have had a long foreground somewhere, for such a start. I rubbed my eyes a little, to see if this sunbeam were no illusion; but the solid sense of the book is a sober certainty. It has the best merits, namely, of fortifying and encouraging.

I did not know until I, last night, saw the book advertised in a newspaper, that I could trust the name as real and available for a Post-office. I wish to see my benefactor, and have felt much like striking my tasks, and visiting New York to pay you my respects.
Concord, Massachusetts, July 21, 1855
—R.W. Emerson

Emerson's letter gave Whitman one of the most remarkable sendoffs in the history of American literature. It has been reprinted or quoted ever since by Walt's followers. It went directly to what Walt had tried to achieve. And it was the best notice Walt got in his lifetime.

For weeks Walt treasured the letter, confiding its praise to no one. Then in September, the Association of New York Publishers held a meeting in New York to which scores of authors, major and minor, were invited—but not Whitman. No one at the meeting mentioned him or his book.

Well, if no one else would beat the drums for *Leaves of Grass*, he would. He used the Emerson letter in a publicity campaign. Somehow the letter appeared in the *New York Tribune*, though no one had asked Emerson's permission. Then Walt himself wrote three unsigned reviews of his own book (favorable of course!) and managed to get them printed in friendly newspapers. Later he had those reviews used for promotion in other contexts. (Not an uncommon practice then—and later, too. Theater producers and book publishers paid the press to run puffs for their products.)

One of Walt's own reviews began, "An American bard at last!" Published in the *United States Review*, Walt's piece centered on the theme of his *Leaves*—America's need for unity, for cultural togetherness. The poet's special role was to bring people together, he said: "He does not separate the learned from the unlearned, the northerner from the southerner, the white from the black, or the native from the immigrant just landed at the wharf."

But was anybody listening? The nation was split by sectionalism, class conflict, political hatreds. Could poetry unify it?

Of the early reviews of Walt's book about half were positive, a quarter mixed, and the rest negative. European reviewers saw *Leaves* as outlandish, reflecting the weird

American culture. One reviewer called it "rubbish" in bad need of weeding. Another, "a mass of stupid filth." A London paper said Whitman was "a startling creation of the modern American mind, but he is no fool."

Chapter 11

The Greatest Democrat

THE REVIEWS, HOWEVER DISAPPROVING, did not cause Walt to drop his pen. He kept on writing poems. In less than a year he produced twenty new ones and revisions of some already published.

His mind was set on a second edition of *Leaves*. But not with any optimism that this one would do better. His notebook tells us he was depressed: "Everything I have done seems to me blank and suspicious . . . my love gets no response . . . I am filled with restlessness . . . " It was a gloominess that would never quite lift.

As the 1850s rolled on, his faith in a resurgent and united democracy faded. Both the economic and political systems looked uglier and uglier. He spoke of the men elected to the White House as this "poor scum." In Kansas, pro- and anti-slavery forces were killing each other. On the Senate floor a Southerner caned abolition Senator Charles Sumner nearly to death. Walt still dreamed of some kind of settlement that would pull the nation together. If not political, then cultural. He looked to the "bravery, friendship, conscientiousness, clear-sightedness and practical genius" of ordinary Americans to link the nation together.

It was in this mood that in 1856 he published the second edition of his book. The first had twelve poems; this one had thirty-two. On the cover was the title, Walt's name, and Emerson's words: "I Greet You at the Beginning of a Great Career." Inside, he printed all of Emerson's letter, without asking permission. The volume was big—384 pages—and priced cheaply, at one dollar.

This time Walt made *Leaves* more appealing to the reader. He gave titles to each of the poems, and numbered them consecutively. He dropped the use of ellipses and went back to more conventional punctuation. He even used a regular metric pattern in some poems in his hunt for popular favor.

Again, sales were small. Comfort came, however, in visits from Concord neighbors of Emerson. Bronson Alcott, the educator, dropped by the Whitman home in Brooklyn. He went for a walk with Walt, then ate a dinner prepared by Walt's mother. While Walt stretched out on a couch Alcott did most of the talking. A month later Alcott returned, this time with Thoreau. Alcott observed that Whitman and Thoreau acted warily, "like two beasts, each wondering what the other would do, whether to snap or run." Walt said he lived to make his poems and "for nothing else particularly." He spent his mornings reading and writing and his afternoons walking—a program much like Thoreau's. Walt gave Thoreau a copy of the new edition of *Leaves*. Later Thoreau wrote a friend that he thought *Leaves* was "an incomparable sermon . . . a great primitive poem, an alarm or trumpet-note ringing through the American camp. . . . By his heartiness and broad generalities he puts me into a liberal frame of mind prepared to see wonders. . . . He is apparently the greatest democrat the world has seen."

About the sensual passages in *Leaves*, Thoreau said Whitman "has spoken more truth than any American or modern that I know. I have found his poem exhilarating, encouraging. . . .We ought to rejoice greatly in him."

In some nine months after the second *Leaves* appeared, Walt wrote seventy new poems. He was looking forward to a third edition. But no publisher was ready to issue another edition. Any number of hopeful writers were working at that time. Yet almost none earned enough to live on. Even one of the most successful, Washington Irving, received just

$204,000 for more than fifty years of arduous literary labor. That was $4,000 a year, the wages of a chief clerk.

Desperate for money, Walt had to go back to journalism. In 1857 he took on the job of editing the *Brooklyn Daily Times*, one of the best papers in the city. He could not look to his father for support, for Mr. Whitman had died in 1855, a week after *Leaves* appeared.

Walt filled the *Times* with sensational news and serial fiction. He catered to the mass hunger for sensationalism while lamenting it in his editorials. His editorials show how disillusioned he had become about the prospects of American democracy. He could not stand the evils of urban society—corruption of business and government, brutal street gangs, drunkenness. "A general laxity of morals," he wrote, "a general indifference to the old standards of right and wrong, by which our fathers regulated their lives, pervades all classes."

He became so disgusted with the corruption he saw around him that his editorials began to read like those found in Southern papers holding up plantation life as a model of cooperative, peaceful labor. In May 1858 Walt supported an Oregon bill to bar blacks from the state. He wrote that blacks and whites could never get along because nature was against it. "Besides, is not America for the Whites? And is it not better so?" Like many others at that time, he thought it better to remove blacks to "some secure and ample part of the earth, where they have a chance to develop themselves, to gradually form a race, a nation, that would take no mean rank among the peoples of the world."

That was the view of the American Colonization Society, which for decades had argued for the removal of blacks to foreign lands. Harriet Beecher Stowe and other Abolitionists endorsed it. And so too, for their own reasons, did such African Americans as Martin Delany and Henry Highland Garnet, who wanted their people to be free and independent in their own country. Lincoln, too, until the Civil War was well under way, believed that freed blacks should be relocated outside the United States. Such thinking was behind the Dred Scott decision of the Supreme Court, which in 1857 denied citizenship to blacks.

In June 1859 Walt left the *Times*, forced out because of conflicts with the owner over controversial editorials. Details of what followed are too scarce for certainty. He earned six or seven dollars a week writing short pieces for other local papers, and was paid small sums on the sale of the third edition of *Leaves*. His family life was troubling. Always short of money, the Whitmans had to rent out their upper floor and live in the basement.

Walt's health declined, probably from hypertension; some think because of a failed love affair. Whether with a man or a woman is not known. The emotional upheaval is treated in a cluster of twelve poems Walt wrote in 1859. Called "Calamus," it appeared in the third edition of *Leaves*, in 1860. That edition was published by a Boston firm, Thayer and Eldridge. Walt hoped to go on with them, but the company failed by the year's end.

Walt had no savings to carry him over to another job. He was casual about money, that is, for himself. When he had some, he helped his family. At one time, while working as an editor, he co-signed the mortgage on the family's house and paid the living expenses for all. At another time he managed a building concern that his father and two brothers worked for.

This was a time when the disunion Walt had long feared seemed imminent. The South was threatening to secede from the Union if Abraham Lincoln, the candidate of the new Republican Party, was elected. Walt and his family had long been Democrats. But when the Republican Party was formed in 1854, they had switched to the new party.

The election campaign was a bitter one. On November 6, 1860, Lincoln won the White House. He had a majority of the electoral vote but only 40 percent of the popular vote. (The rest was divided among the three other candidates.)

On his way to Washington to be inaugurated, Lincoln stopped in New York to stay overnight at the Astor House, opposite City Hall Park. He stepped out of the horse-drawn carriage to stretch his arms and legs. As he looked out over the huge crowd of 30–40,000 people, there was an unbroken silence. Walt said he had a great view of Mr. Lincoln—"his perfect composure and coolness, his unusual and uncouth height, his dress of complete black, stovepipe hat pushed back on the head, dark-brown complexion, seamed and wrinkled yet canny-looking face, black, bushy head of hair, disproportionately long neck, and his hands held behind him as he stood observing the people. He looked with curiosity upon that immense sea of faces, and the sea of faces returned the look with similar curiosity."

Six weeks after the Lincoln victory, South Carolina withdrew from the Union, adopting a flag of its own and taking over all federal buildings in the state. Within a few weeks, many other Southern states withdrew, declaring that under the doctrine of states rights, they had a right to do it.

In February 1861, at Montgomery, Alabama, the seceders established the "Confederate States of America" and elected Jefferson Davis of Mississippi president.

News of the Confederate bombardment of Fort Sumter in Charleston harbor reached New York late on the night of April 13, 1861. Immediately the news was headlined on extras that sped through the streets. Toward midnight, Walt was walking down Broadway after leaving a performance of a Verdi opera when he heard the loud cries of newsboys tearing down the street. He bought an extra and stopped at the Metropolitan Hotel, where a crowd was gathering, reading the news. For those who had no paper someone read aloud the telegram announcing the attack. They stood silent a minute or two, before they dispersed. In the next days Walt felt that only a few in the North realized how grave was this threat to national authority. Contempt, anger, disbelief that such a rebellion could occur. "It'll blow over in sixty days," many said.

Would it? Walt wrote a recruiting poem, "Beat! Beat! Drums!":

> To the drum-taps prompt,
> The young men falling in and arming,
> The mechanics arming (the trowel, the jack-plane, the
>   blacksmith's hammer, tost aside with precipitation),
> The lawyer leaving his office and arming, the judge leaving
>   the court,
> The driver deserting his wagon in the street, jumping
>   down, throwing the reins abruptly down on the horses'
>   backs,
> The salesman leaving the store, the boss, book-keeper,
>   porter, all leaving;
> Squads gather everywhere by common consent and arm,
> The new recruits, even boys, the old men show them how
>   to wear their accoutrements, they buckle the straps
>   carefully,
> Outdoors arming, indoors arming, the flash of musket-
>   barrels,
> The white tents cluster in camps, the arm'd sentries
>   around, the sunrise cannon and again at sunset,

New York regiment fighting in the first battle of Bull
Run, July 21, 1861

94

Arm'd regiments arrive every day, pass through the city,
    and embark from the wharves, [...]
The tearful parting, the mother kisses her son, the son
    kisses his mother, [...]
The artillery, the silent cannons bright as gold, drawn
    along, rumble lightly over the stones, ...
The hospital service, the lint, bandages and medicines,
The women volunteering for nurses, the work begun for in
    earnest, no more parade now [...]

Then came the terrible shock on July 21 of the battle of
Bull Run. Each side supposed it had won, till the last
moment, when the Union troops exploded in a panic and
fled from the battlefield.

The Civil War would last four years, from April 1861 to
April 1865. When it began, the balance of forces was very
uneven, with the North far stronger in manpower, industry,
agriculture, and finance; a railroad system linking all its
parts; and a good merchant marine.

How could the South think it could win? Because it had
contempt for the North and blind pride in itself. The North
wouldn't put up a real fight. The South had only to stand
strong on the defensive and the North would get sick of los-
ing battles and quit.

The defeat at Bull Run scared the North. If the Rebels
could do so well, the capital at Washington was itself in danger. Lincoln had called for three-month volunteers, but after
Bull Run he realized that to invade the South he needed a
larger and more permanent and better-trained army. Walt,
then forty-two, was too old for combat. His brother George,
thirty-two, joined up and became an officer in a New York
regiment. One day Walt saw in a newspaper that his brother

Walt's younger brother, George Whitman, photographed
after he volunteered in the Union army

was among those listed as seriously wounded in the savage
battle of Fredericksburg on December 13, 1862.

He hurried south to see if he could be of any help.

Chapter 12

A Great Slaughterhouse

O N DECEMBER 19, 1862, WALT FOUND his brother at the army hospital at Falmouth, Virginia. He was relieved to learn George had suffered only a minor face wound. But what Walt saw in the nine days he stayed there shook him terribly:

> Outdoors, at the foot of a tree, I notice a heap of amputated feet, legs, arms, hands, etc. a full load for a one-horse cart. Several dead bodies lie near, each covered with its brown woolen blanket. In the dooryard are fresh graves, mostly of officers, their names on pieces of barrel staves or broken boards, stuck in the dirt.

He entered a house taken over for a hospital. All the rooms were crowded with wounded soldiers, both Union and Rebel, the wounds pretty bad, some frightful, the men in their old clothes, unclean and bloody. Some were dying, "I had nothing to give at that visit, but wrote a few letters to folks home, mothers, etc. Also talked to three or four needing it."

The sight would haunt him, as a symbol of the American union dismembered, as were the bodies of its men. It reminded him of the cattle-pens of New York—"a great slaughterhouse and the men mutually butchering each other . . . "

That brief glimpse of human destruction caused Walt to write his first important poem about the war: "A Sight in Camp in the Daybreak Gray and Dim."

> A sight in camp in the daybreak gray and dim,
> As from my tent I emerge so early sleepless,
> As slow I walk in the cool fresh air the path near by the
>   hospital tent,

Union troops, the sick and the wounded,
await medical treatment in Virginia

Three forms I see on stretchers lying, brought out there
    untended lying,
Over each the blanket spread, ample brownish woolen
    blanket,
Gray and heavy blanket, folding, covering all.

Curious I halt and silent stand,
Then with light fingers I from the face of the nearest the
    first just lift the blanket;

99

Who are you elderly man so gaunt and grim, with well-
 gray'd hair, and flesh all sunken about the eyes?
Who are you my dear comrade?

Then to the second I step—and who are you my child and
 darling?
Who are you sweet boy with cheeks yet blooming?
Then to the third—a face nor child nor old, very calm, as of
 beautiful yellow-white ivory;
Young man I think I know you—I think this face is the face
 of the Christ himself,
Dear and divine and brother of all, and here again he lies.

The Civil War was awesomely destructive. Military technology had rushed far ahead of military tactics and medical treatment. An immense number of amputations were done without anesthesia. Because the wounded lay on the battlefield for long hours and even days before they could be carried off, infections and gangrene were common. More soldiers died in that war than in all other American wars together.

The shock of those amputated arms and legs roused in Walt a sense of what he must do. He began almost at once to visit the wounded in the battleground's field hospitals. "I go around from one case to another," he wrote in his notebook. "I do not see that I do much good to these wounded and dying; but I cannot leave them."

The battle George had fought in caused thousands of casualties on both sides, hundreds dying every day as Walt stayed on. Most of the wounded lay in tents—poor ones—on blankets spread on layers of twigs or leaves. No cots, seldom even a mattress, the ground frozen hard, and snow filtering in. As he moved about, "once in a while some youngster holds on to me convulsively, and I do what I can for him; at any rate, stop with him and sit near him for hours, if he wishes it."

In December he left the camp at Falmouth and with a transport of wounded men moved on up to Washington. For the next three years he would act as nurse, helper, friend to the wounded, sick, and dying soldiers in the hospital wards of Washington. It was a way of ministering to the wounded body of the republic, almost literally. Later, in his notebook, he summed up that time:

> During those three years in hospital, camp or field, I made over six hundred visits or tours, and went, as I estimate, counting all, among from eighty thousand to a hundred thousand of the wounded and sick, as sustainer of spirit and body in some degree, in time of need. These visits varied from an hour or two, to all day or night; for with dear or critical cases I generally watch'd all night. Sometimes I took up my quarters in the hospital, and slept and watch'd there several nights in succession. Those three years I consider the greatest privilege and satisfaction, (with all their feverish excitements and physical deprivations and lamentable sights,) and, of course, the most profound lesson of my life. I can say that in my ministerings I comprehended all, whoever came in my way, northern or southern, and slighted none. It arous'd and brought out and decided undream'd-of depths of emotion. It has given me my most fervent views of the true ensemble and extent of the States . . .
>
> I was with many rebel officers and men among our wounded, and gave them always what I had, and tried to cheer them same as any. I was among the army teamsters considerably, and, indeed, always found myself drawn to them. Among the black soldiers, wounded or

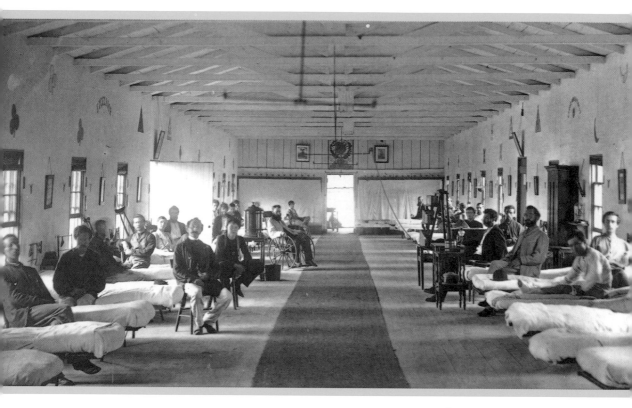

Ward patients in the Armory Square Hospital,
where Whitman made his daily rounds bringing gifts
and comfort to the soldiers

sick, and in the contraband camps, I also took my way
whenever in their neighborhood, and did what I could
for them.

Determined to stay in Washington for the duration,
Walt found part-time work as a clerk in the army paymaster's office. An anti-slavery novelist he had met before the
war, William O'Connor, and his wife, Ellen, rented him a

small room in their apartment on L Street. They became close friends, and together with other Washingtonians shared a lively social life. He lived mostly on bread and tea so that he could spend what little he earned on the wounded soldiers. He visited the hospital almost every day, and often at night, too. Those hours, day after day, year after year, nursing young men from all the states, North and South, would bring Walt to the heart of America.

Rising early each day he would scrub himself clean, dress, have his meager breakfast, stuff a knapsack with gifts for the soldiers, go to his office and then, when work was done, move on to the hospitals. In Ward F, for instance, his notebook records that he "supplied the men throughout with writing paper and stamped envelope each; a large jar of first-rate preserved berries, donated to me by a lady—her own cooking. Found several cases I thought good subject for small sums of money, which I furnished. The wounded men often come up broke, and it helps the spirits to have even the small sum I give them." He handed around books and papers, oranges, apples, sweet crackers, figs, jellies, wine, brandy, and tobacco, socks, handkerchiefs, underwear. He jotted down each soldier's name, rank, corps, regiment, bed number, ward, hospital, nature of wound or illness, and the name and address of parents and wives. What the men wanted most was writing materials, or, if unable to write home themselves, told Walt what to write.

All this cost money. Walt wangled it wherever he could. He asked old friends and new, and earned something more by writing pieces for newspapers and magazines. When more help was needed in the wards he solicited volunteers.

Sometimes he dressed wounds. But more valuable than medical nursing and gifts were the times when he simply sat

A letter typical of the many Walt wrote to reassure the parents of soldiers he visited in the hospital

Washington
June 10. 1865.

Mr. & Mrs. Pratt:

As I am visiting your son Alfred occasionally, to cheer him up in his sickness in hospital, I thought you might like a few words, though from a stranger, yet a friend to your boy. I was there last night, and sat by his bed, as usual, & saw the letter he had just written. He wrote to you that he had diarrhea pretty bad, but is now improved & getting along well in hospital — but as it was a hot & powerful day, I advised him to keep indoors much at present, as the most is rest, and he will get his strength again.

We are having very hot weather here, & it is dry & dusty.— The City is alive with soldiers from both the Army of the Potomac & the Western Armies, brought here by Sherman. There have been some great Reviews here, as you have seen in the papers — & thousands of soldiers are going home every day.

You must write to Alfred often, as it cheers up a boy sick & away from home. Write all about domestic & farm incidents, and as cheerful as may be. Direct to him, in Ward C. Armory Square Hospital, Washington, D.C. Should any thing occur, I will write you again, but I feel confident he will continue doing well. For the present farewell.

Walt Whitman
Washington
D C

quietly beside a soldier's bed and wrote a letter for him or led him to talk. He learned that the daily offer of friendship and affection could do much to cure the sick and wounded.

After nearly half a year of his hospital rounds, Walt's own health began to fail. Sore throats, headaches, infections picked up from the sick or from cuts suffered when assisting in surgery, and waves of sadness at the pitiful sight every day of shattered youth. And young they were; a great number only fifteen to twenty-one. Still, though plagued with his own physical and emotional troubles, Walt would not give up his commitment.

In summertime Walt would walk through fields and gather great bunches of dandelions and red and white clover, which he scattered over the hospital cots. Sometimes, when he sensed a whole ward full of despair, he would read aloud to break the mood—Shakespeare or the Bible, never his own poems. Or something funny, from one of the popular humorists. Each man needed special attention at times, and he learned to adjust himself to every need, whether trivial or not.

He kept a series of little pocket notebooks, jotting down what he saw or heard or felt as he went along. These became woven into his collection of poems called "Drum-Taps" or into his prose work, *Specimen Days*.

From his poem "The Wound-Dresser" comes this passage telling of his care for the war-wounded:

On, on I go, (open doors of time! open hospital doors!)
The crush'd head I dress (poor crazed hand tear not the
   bandage away),
The neck of the cavalry-man with the bullet through and
   through I examine,
Hard the breathing rattles, quite glazed already the eye, yet
   life struggles hard,

(Come sweet death! Be persuaded O beautiful death!
In mercy come quickly.)

From the stump of the arm, the amputated hand,
I undo the clotted lint, remove the slough, wash off the
  matter and blood,

But in silence, in dreams' projections,
While the world of gain and appearance and mirth goes on,
So soon what is over forgotten, and waves wash the
  imprints off the sand,
With hinged knees returning I enter the doors (while for
  you up there,
Whoever you are, follow without noise and be of strong
  heart).

Bearing the bandages, water and sponge,
Straight and swift to my wounded I go,
Where they lie on the ground after the battle brought in,
Where their priceless blood reddens the grass, the ground,
Or to the rows of the hospital tent, or under the roof'd
  hospital,
To the long rows of cots up and down each side I return,
To each and all one after another I draw near, not one do I
  miss,
An attendant follows holding a tray, he carries a refuse
  pail,
Soon to be fill'd with clotted rags and blood, emptied, and
  fill'd again.
I onward go, I stop,
With hinged knees and steady hand to dress wounds,
I am firm with each, the pangs are sharp yet unavoidable,
One turns to me his appealing eyes—poor boy! I never
  knew you,
Yet I think I could not refuse this moment to die for you, if
  that would save you.

Back on his pillow the soldier bends with curv'd neck and
  side-falling head,
His eyes are closed, his face is pale, he dares not look on
  the bloody stump,
And has not yet look'd on it.

I dress a wound in the side, deep, deep,
But a day or two more, for see the frame all wasted and
  sinking,
And the yellow-blue countenance see.

I dress the perforated shoulder, the foot with the bullet-
  wound,
Cleanse the one with a gnawing and putrid gangrene, so
  sickening, so offensive,
While the attendant stands behind aside me holding the
  tray and pail.

I am faithful, I do not give out,
The fractur'd thigh, the knee, the wound in the abdomen,
These and more I dress with impassive hand (yet deep in
  my breast a fire, a burning flame).

Thus in silence in dreams' projections,
Returning, resuming, I thread my way through the
  hospitals,
The hurt and wounded I pacify with soothing hand,
I sit by the restless all the dark night, some are so young,
Some suffer so much, I recall the experience sweet and sad,
(Many a soldier's loving arms about this neck have cross'd
  and rested,
Many a soldier's kiss dwells on these bearded lips).

Walt liked to wander the streets of the capital at night,
or linger along the moonlit Potomac. He watched the types
who came to Washington to seek work or favors. They
swarmed in the White House and didn't hesitate to accost

the president when he passed in the corridors. He met men drawn to the new profession of war correspondent, and artists like Winslow Homer, visiting the front to draw scenes of the war. One day in 1863, Walt met John Burroughs, a young farmer from the Catskills who worked as a guard in the Treasury building, and who later became nationally famous as a naturalist. Through a long friendship Burroughs came to love Whitman. He would write the first biography of the poet.

On his rambles in the city Walt often came across Lincoln, and wrote this account:

> I see the President almost every day, as I happen to live where he passes to or from his lodgings out of town. He never sleeps at the White House during the hot season, but has quarters at a healthy location some three miles north of the city, the Soldiers' home, a United States military establishment. I saw him this morning about 8 1/2 coming in to business, riding on Vermont avenue, near L street . . . Mr. Lincoln on the saddle generally rides a good-sized, easy-going gray horse, is dress'd in plain black, somewhat rusty and dusty, wears a black stiff hat, and looks about as ordinary in attire, &c., as the commonest man . . .
>
> I see very plainly ABRAHAM LINCOLN'S dark brown face, with the deep-cut lines, the eyes, always to me with a deep latent sadness in the expression. We have got so that we exchange bows, and very cordial ones. Sometimes the President goes and comes in an open barouche. The cavalry always accompany him with drawn sabres. . . . The equipage is of the plainest kind, only two horses, and they nothing extra. They pass'd me once very close, and I saw the President in the face fully, as they were moving slowly, and his look, though

abstracted, happen'd to be directed steadily in my eye. He bow'd and smiled, but far beneath his smile I noticed well the expression I have alluded to. None of the artists or pictures had caught the deep, though subtle and indirect expression of this man's face. There is something else there. One of the great portrait painters of two or three centuries ago is needed.

Carl Sandburg, in his biography of Lincoln, holds that while living in Springfield, Illinois, Lincoln read the second edition of *Leaves of Grass*. His law partner, William Herndon, had bought a copy in 1857 and talked to Lincoln about it. Lincoln borrowed the book, enjoyed it so much that he read passages aloud to friends. Like Whitman, Lincoln was the son of a carpenter and farmer and had tried his hand at poems, too. From their youth both men had come to love Shakespeare and the Bible. Lincoln's superb prose earned him the admiration of the literary world. Both are considered among the great masters of their art—prose and poetry.

Chapter 13

Hell
Itself

A S THE SUMMER OF 1863 BEGAN, Walt's friends, the O'Connors, had to move, leaving him without their daily companionship. Alone now, he gave even more time to his hospital visits. It only deepened his blues. Day after day, death and suffering multiplied as the battles went on endlessly. Wounded men he had come to love recovered and went back to their units, or if too weak, were sent home. And the rest—they died.

Walt barely survived the anguish. In bed at night, recalling the dead and dying, he would feel sick and tremble uncontrollably. He learned to keep himself mindlessly busy to stop the flow of tears.

In October 1863 Walt moved into new quarters, on Sixth Street. It was a single room tucked under the roof of a three-story house, with a good view south. A month later he took the train to New York, arriving home in Brooklyn. He had been gone over ten months, and found the family eager to hear of his experiences in Washington. He went out often with old friends—eating, drinking, laughing, talking. But after a few weeks of partying he had enough. He could not forget the faces of the sick and wounded.

Back in Washington, Walt spent New Year's Eve with the O'Connors and other friends, sipping hot toddies and talking about anything and everything till midnight, when all went home—to wake the next morning to an even bloodier year than 1863.

In February, hoping to be present at a "first-class battle," Walt interrupted his hospital visits to accompany his paymaster chief to the winter camp of the Army of the Potomac. Here, too, the field hospitals were only a collection of tents with the bare ground their floor. There was a great deal of diarrhea, so awful a complaint that many died of it. Later, Walt said the war had been "about nine hundred ninety-nine parts diarrhea to one part glory."

Returning to the hospital wards, Walt found the whole city awaiting an attack on Lee's army by General U.S. Grant. On May 5 the Battle of the Wilderness began. The fighting, lasting two days, was the worst ever. A Southerner called it "butchery pure and simple," while a Union colonel said "It seemed as though Christian men had turned to fiends, and hell itself had usurped the place of earth." The cost to Grant's army was a frightful 17,500 casualties.

On June 12, another battle ended, at Cold Harbor, with 7,000 men lost in eight minutes. In four weeks 65,000 soldiers had been killed or wounded, or 60 percent of all Union troops during the three previous years. "I cannot bear it," said Lincoln. "This suffering, this loss of life is dreadful."

As the wounded flooded into the hospitals Walt felt almost unable to take it anymore. "It is awful to see so much, and not be able to relieve it." By mid-June he had become so sick that the doctors ordered him to stay away from the hospitals altogether. His symptoms were so many and so complex that no one could be sure what the chief trouble was. With all that terrible stress, it may have been partly psychosomatic. He did not want to leave, but in late June was so badly off he had to return to Brooklyn.

Once home with the family, however, he rapidly improved. How he endured his hospital work as long as he did is a wonder.

At home, and while still in bed recovering, Walt began to prepare for publication the war poems composed in Washington. As his health improved, he looked up old friends, made the rounds of favorite hangouts, went to political ral-

Whitman in the war years, revealing how
the stress of his hospital work had aged him

lies, and visited his sisters in Vermont and on Long Island.
Meanwhile, brother George had miraculously survived years
of combat without any further injuries. Then, in late September 1863, his regiment was overrun by Confederates and

he was taken prisoner. An article Walt wrote about George's New York regiment marching and fighting for three years was printed in *The New York Times*.

Five days later Walt went to the polls and voted for Lincoln in the 1864 election. The President was reelected, partly because of a flood of absentee ballots from soldiers at the front.

Walt kept trying to find a publisher for *Drum-Taps*, his war poems, but without success. Six months had passed since returning home; he was ready to pick up his commitment in Washington. William O'Connor found a job for him in the Department of the Interior. It would provide a steady income and the hours needed for his hospital visits. Classified as a clerk first-class, he would be paid a salary of $1,200 a year, a huge break for a man used to living on a few dollars a week. His assignment was to the Bureau of Indian Affairs, located in the basement of the U.S. Patent Office.

Walt began work in late January 1865. He found a room, and resumed the hospital visits for a few hours daily plus all day Sundays. He tried not to overdo it, fearing a nervous breakdown. On March 4, Inauguration Day, Walt caught sight of the President riding in a carriage with his son Tad by his side. He thought that Lincoln looked "very much worn and tired, the lines indeed of vast responsibilities, intricate questions, and demands of life and death, cut deeper than ever upon his dark brown face; yet with all the old goodness, tenderness, sadness, and canny shrewdness underneath the furrows."

That evening Walt joined the large crowd entering the White House to congratulate the President. He watched as both Mr. and Mrs. Lincoln welcomed people on the receiving line. It would be his last look at the man he had come to love.

"O Captain!"

Oddly, Whitman's best known poem—"O Captain! My Captain!"—is the one he detested. About the death of Lincoln, its sing-song rhyme has been memorized and recited by pupils for generations, and anthologized in school readers. Critics have called it "a piece of melodramatic doggerel." Walt himself, near the end of his life, said he was sorry he ever wrote it, for it had become far better known than one of his greatest poems, "When Lilacs Last in the Dooryard Bloom'd."

Two weeks later, given a furlough from his job, Walt went home to Brooklyn. He wanted to spend time with his brother George, just released from six months of starvation and humiliation in a Confederate prison camp. Walt published his account of George's experience in the *Brooklyn Daily Union*. Then, on April 1, Walt contracted with a New York printer to bring out 500 copies of *Drum-Taps*, containing forty-seven new poems. While Walt was still at home, news came of the fall of Richmond and Lee's surrender to Grant. The war was over. There were raucous celebrations all over the North, but, like his brother George, Walt was simply too worn down to join in.

Home with his mother on April 15, Walt picked up the daily newspaper to read the shocking news that Lincoln was dead. On April 14 the President and his wife had gone to see a play at Ford's Theater in Washington. During the performance John Wilkes Booth shot the President. Lincoln died the next morning without ever regaining consciousness.

The Whitmans were stunned. They got through the morning silently, drinking cups of coffee, eating nothing, watching for the newspaper extras to land on their doorstep. The assassin, a handsome actor, was the son of that famous Junius Brutus Booth whom Walt had admired so greatly as an intuitive artist who had broken the formal tradition of stage acting—as Walt would do with poetry.

That afternoon Walt took the ferry to Manhattan and walked along Broadway to find shops shuttered, flags at half-mast, the streets nearly deserted. Everywhere he sensed a "strange mixture of horror, fury, tenderness and a stirring of wonder." By the next day he began to think of the martyred president as the one man who must be seen as the conservator of the Union. "Yes, he was assassinated—but the Union is not assassinated . . . the Nation is immortal."

He decided to hold up printing *Drum-Taps* until he could find the way to express his grief. He returned to Washington, where spring was well advanced and the lilacs in full bloom. "I find myself always reminded of the great tragedy of that day by the sight and color of these blossoms. It never fails." Although he had not seen Lincoln's funeral cortege back to Springfield, Illinois, the press had reported that great sprays of lilacs covered Lincoln's coffin.

Slowly, an elegy began to form in his mind. He found in Venus, the western star, the symbol of Lincoln, the Westerner. The lilac, the most familiar dooryard flower, symbolized the poet's love for Lincoln. And in the song of the hermit thrush, he heard the murmuring chant of death:

When Lilacs Last in the Dooryard Bloom'd

1

When lilacs last in the dooryard bloom'd,
And the great star early droop'd in the western sky in the
    night,
I mourn'd, and yet shall mourn with ever-returning spring.

Ever-returning spring, trinity sure to me you bring,
Lilac blooming perennial and drooping star in the west,
And thought of him I love.

2

O powerful western fallen star!
O shades of night—O moody, tearful night!
O great star disappear'd—O the black murk that hides the
    star!
O cruel hands that hold me powerless—O helpless soul of
    me!
O harsh surrounding cloud that will not free my soul.

3

In the dooryard fronting an old farm-house near the white-
    wash'd palings,
Stands the lilac-bush tall-growing with heart-shaped leaves
    of rich green,
With many a pointed blossom rising delicate, with the per-
    fume strong I love,
With every leaf a miracle—and from this bush in the door-
    yard,
With delicate-color'd blossoms and heart-shaped leaves of
    rich green,
A sprig with its flower I break.

4

In the swamp in secluded recesses,
A shy and hidden bird is warbling a song.

Solitary the thrush,
The hermit withdrawn to himself, avoiding the settlements,
Sings by himself a song.

Song of the bleeding throat,
Death's outlet song of life, (for well, dear brother, I know,
If thou wast not granted to sing thou would'st surely die).

5

Over the breast of the spring, the land, amid cities,
Amid lanes and through old woods, where lately the violets
    peep'd from the ground, spotting the gray debris,
Amid the grass in the fields each side of the lanes, passing
    the endless grass,
Passing the yellow-spear'd wheat, every grain from its
    shroud in the dark-brown fields uprisen,
Passing the apple-tree blows of white and pink in the
    orchards,
Carrying a corpse to where it shall rest in the grave,
Night and day journeys a coffin.

6

Coffin that passes through lanes and streets,
Through day and night with the great cloud darkening the
    land,
With the pomp of the inloop'd flags with the cities draped
    in black,
With the show of the States themselves as of crape-veil'd
    women standing,

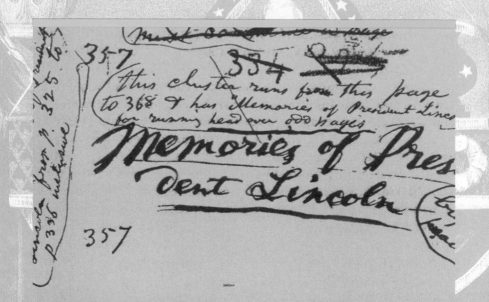

WHEN LILACS LAST IN THE DOOR-YARD BLOOM'D

1

WHEN lilacs last in the door-yard bloom'd,
And the great star early droop'd in the western sky in
the night,
I mourn'd—and yet shall mourn with ever-returning
spring.

O ever-returning spring, trinity sure to me you
bring,
Lilac blooming perennial, and drooping star in the
west,
And thought of him I love.

2

O powerful, western, fallen star!
O shades of night! O moody, tearful night!
O great star disappear'd! O the black murk that hides
the star!
O cruel hands that hold me powerless! O helpless soul
of me!
O harsh surrounding cloud, that will not free my soul!

Manuscript revision of
When Lilacs Last in the Dooryard Bloom'd

With processions long and winding and the flambeaus of
    the night,
With the countless torches lit, with the silent sea of faces
    and the unbared heads,
With the waiting depot, the arriving coffin, and the sombre
    faces,
With dirges through the night, with the shout and voices
    rising strong and solemn,
With all the mournful voices of the dirges pour'd around
    the coffin,
The dim-lit churches and the shuddering organs—where
    amid these you journey,
With the tolling, tolling bells' perpetual clang,
Here, coffin that slowly passes,
I give you my sprig of lilac . . .

Chapter 14

A New United States?

I N JUNE, WALT LOST HIS JOB AT THE Bureau of Indian Affairs when a new Secretary of the Interior decided Whitman's poetry set a bad moral example for government clerks. Only a day later a friend found Walt another job, in the Attorney General's office.

What helped Walt's reputation then, and continues to do so, was a pamphlet called *The Good Gray Poet* (1866). It was a tribute to Walt's devoted service to the Civil War soldiers, written by his friend William O'Connor. That service continued, for Walt remained faithful to his volunteer work until the last Civil War hospital closed in April 1866.

"It was a religion with me," he said later. "Every man has a religion . . . something which absorbs him, possesses itself of him, makes him over in its image . . . That, whatever it is, seized upon me, made me its servant, slave; induced me to set aside other ambitions: a trail of glory in the heavens, which I followed, followed with a full heart."

As a journalist, Walt had witnessed such greed and corruption in the worlds of business and politics that it disgusted him. In the hospital wards he found a different America. Caring for the sick, wounded, and dying soldiers he saw in them the courage and decency of the people who "proved humanity," he said, and "proved America."

Throughout his Lincoln elegy you can feel Walt's faith in the American people. Yes, the nation had split in two. But now was the time for reconciliation. The warring brothers would unite again; he was sure of it.

The dream of reconciliation would not happen. Not then, not for decades to come. The violence that ended Lincoln's life would go on to persecute millions—the African Americans. For the majority of the American people were not ready to integrate black people into a free and equal life.

Nor was Walt. He was all for universal suffrage, only in his mind that did not include African Americans. He, like so many others, was an easy victim to the ex-Confederates' propaganda against "Negro rule" in the defeated South.

With the end of the Civil War, the era of Reconstruction began. A new United States was being born out of the old, and people and parties tried to mold its shape, from Northern abolitionists at one end to ex-Confederate officials at the other. For a time the former slaveholders held onto power, but then Congress rejected their plans. It adopted the Thirteenth, Fourteenth, and Fifteenth Amendments to the Constitution that assured blacks of all the rights every citizen was entitled to, including full citizenship. Southerners resisted the basic change with terror and intimidation. The U.S. armed forces had to be sent into the South to enforce the law.

Walt played a part, though a minor one, in those events. He remained in the Attorney General's office from 1865 to 1873, when a paralytic stroke forced him to retire. In those years he shocked friends with his defense of President Andrew Johnson's trying to re-establish the slaveholders' control of the South. When Johnson (himself a former slaveholder) issued pardons wholesale to thousands of ex-Confederates it left the freed people at the mercy of the rebels. Walt's job as record clerk was to process those pardons.

His racist-minded superiors called Walt "a very kind, friendly fellow," and he said, "I couldn't wish to have better bosses."

While Walt helped the reactionary President Johnson, he damned those who fought for civil rights in the Congress and in the country. One possible reason is that himself a man of humble origin, he saw the self-made President as a folk hero whose oratorical powers had carried him all the way up to the White House,

During the Reconstruction era, Walt's writings, both poetry and prose, revealed his anxiety about the harm black liberation might do to the nation. Although he had protested against the inhumanity of slavery and the slave trade, he continued to share in the popular prejudice against blacks.

Walt had hoped the effect of the Civil War would be to strengthen and expand democracy. Instead he saw an America transformed from a nation of farmers and independent craftsmen into an industrial society of mass-production workers, factory owners, and business tycoons. Millions of men, women, and children left their farms and villages for the low wages and long hours of work in the cities. A flood tide of immigrants joined them to labor in the mines, factories, and sweatshops and to live in company towns and slum tenements.

In those closing decades of the nineteenth century, working people rose up to organize unions in their own defense, not only to secure higher wages and safer working conditions, but to demand basic respect for the dignity of the worker.

Walt observed with dismay the rise of the great "captains of industry"—such men as Andrew Carnegie, Philip Armour, James Hill, Jay Gould, Jim Fisk, John D. Rockefeller, and J. P. Morgan. These men formed "the new nobility of industry and banking" that dominated almost every aspect of American life. Attaining material wealth became the highest goal of life. The desire for money and still more money possessed almost all Americans.

It was Mark Twain who gave the era the name that stuck—The Gilded Age—the title he used for his satiric novel about the era.

From the Civil War on, business grew larger and larger, and as the money power merged with the industrial power, it grew more unified. Monopoly—the domination or control of a whole industry such as steel or oil by one company—took hold.

Working as a clerk in Washington for a petty income, Walt noted what was happening to his America. "The depravity of the business classes of our country," he wrote in 1871, "is not less than has been supposed, but infinitely greater. The official services of America, national, state and municipal, in all their branches, except the judiciary, are saturated in corruption, bribery, falsehood, mal-administration, and the judiciary is tainted. The great cities reek with respectable as much as non-respectable robbery and scoundrelism."

Walt saw how money was being worshipped. "Democracy looks with suspicious, ill-satisfied eyes upon the very poor, the ignorant, and on those out of business. She asks for men and women with occupations, well-off owners of houses and acres, and with cash in the bank." Maybe he heard of one millionaire of the 1880s who said defiantly, "We are the rich; we own America; we got it, God knows how, but we intend to keep it if we can."

If Walt once wrote poems in praise of democratic individualism, he now saw what little concern it had for communal responsibility. These politicians and businessmen "with hearts of rags and souls of chalk—are these worth preaching for and dying upon the cross?"

In 1871, Walt published an eighty-four-page pamphlet called "Democratic Vistas." It combined three of his pub-

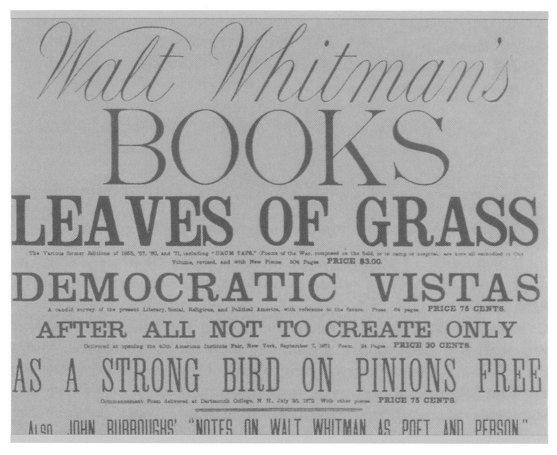

Broadside advertising poster written
by Whitman for his books

lished essays on the problems and contradictions of democracy in America. They were a mixture of a realistic view of politics with a poet's vision of democracy, evolving in the end to a dynamic unity. Our problems, he said, "now include lack of leadership, false standards of value, sugar-coated delusions . . . "

"Song of Myself"

In the first edition of *Leaves of Grass*, the poem called "Song of Myself" occupies more than half the book. This short passage is taken as an expression of Walt's disgust with the selfish, immoral way—scarcely human—that some people live:

> I think I could turn and live with animals, they are so
>   placid and self contain'd,
> I stand and look at them long and long.
>
> They do not sweat and whine about their condition,
> They do not lie awake in the dark and weep for their
>   sins,
> They do not make me sick discussing their duty to
>   God,
> Not one is dissatisfied, not one is demented with the
>   mania of owning things,
> Not one kneels to another, nor to his kind that lived
>   thousands of years ago,
> Not one is respectable or unhappy over the whole
>   earth.

The Whitman scholar Betsy Erkkila says Walt "was one of the first major writers to chart the potentially downward spiral of American history in the postwar years . . . one of the first to grapple with the problems not only of democracy but also of machine technology, incorporation, modernization, and unlimited production that would mark the twenti-eth century." Great poets were needed, Walt believed, to cre-ate a new state of mind that would bring about a total trans-formation of American life. Only poets could provide the language and the myths through which America would find its true self.

Chapter 15

Hymn
to the
Modern Age

WALT, TOO, WAS CHANGING, JUST AS the nation at large was changing. Late in 1865 he published *Drum-Taps*, a volume of fifty-three poems that were mostly patriotic, and often conservative in form to please popular taste. Reviewers noted the changes and praised the poet for avoiding the "indecency" of sexual themes.

A year later friend John Burroughs published an essay on Whitman, the first detailed and most influential appraisal of the poet. No wonder it gave Walt a great boost: He had ghost-written part of it himself. Walt's poetry, Burroughs wrote, "means power, health, freedom, democracy, self-esteem, a full life in the open air, an escape from old forms and standards." And then, to fix in the public mind a happy image, he depicted the poet as having "a large, summery, motherly soul that shines in all his ways and looks."

The next year Burroughs expanded the essay into a book called *Notes on Walt Whitman, As Poet and Person*. Burroughs said Walt was totally neglected, a sentimental appeal for support that was hardly true.

Walt liked this portrait that he helped fashion, and for the rest of his life he would shape his looks and behavior to mirror it. He even let it influence the issue of censorship. In 1868 the first edition of his work not directly under his control appeared, edited by the British poet William Michael Rossetti. The new edition left out large parts of some of his major poems and even "Song of Myself." But Walt, eager for recognition and sales, let the butchered edition go through. It was an example of behavior that would follow: cries of rebellion and then compromise or surrender.

A Poet's Living

What did a poet earn? Whitman complained about the difficulty of making a living, but the record shows that he didn't do so badly. In 1875 the average annual wage of the American worker was about $800. That was for working a ten-hour day, and often longer. From that time until his death in 1892, Walt's income was $1,270 per year. He held no job in those seventeen years. The money came from book royalties, magazine and lecture fees, and contributions from friends and admirers. When he died, his bank savings amounted to $7,379.02.

Still, his earnings were way below what the popular writers of the day enjoyed.

Still, Walt's religious belief, and his faith in Darwinian evolution, led him to see history as a long-developing process through which, however slowly, good would triumph over evil. And so, too, with his own work: *Leaves of Grass* he said, "is evolution—evolution in its most varied, freest, largest sense."

As old age crept up on him, Walt's view of capitalism and of businessmen softened. He knew the harm done working people by the almost demonic passion for profit. At the same time, in the long view, he believed the profit system would bring prosperity to the nation as a whole. That aspect of Whitman's thought won him the admiration of such business tycoons as Andrew Carnegie, who called him America's greatest poet.

Walt's health had begun to fail during the war years. Bouts of dizziness, faintness, infections weakened him. Doctors couldn't trace the cause of his symptoms. Adding to the pressure were family troubles—lack of money, misbehavior, accidents, death—things he couldn't do much about, but which were painful to endure.

As technology made dazzling advances in the decades following the war, Walt celebrated the achievements in his poetry. Technological breakthroughs were knitting the world together, he thought. The Suez Canal had opened, the railroad had spanned the North American continent, the Atlantic cable had snaked beneath the ocean to link Europe with America. These "modern wonders," Walt said, will make possible an age of universal peace and brotherhood. "Passage to India," a nine-section poem, is his hymn to the modern age. It places the poet as partner to scientist and engineer, moving toward a time when human conflict will disappear and spiritual unity will be achieved.

Walt himself thought this poem was his best postwar work: "There's more of me, the essential ultimate me, in that than in any of the poems."

In 1871, Walt was paid a hundred dollars to write a poem for the National Industrial Exposition and to read it before an audience in New York. They applauded him warmly and many newspapers printed the poem. Unlike his earlier "A Song for Occupations," which valued the individual worker, "Song of the Exposition" pays tribute to the modern technology that multiplies the power of the anonymous workforce.

In January 1873, Walt suffered a stroke that paralyzed his left side. It took three months before he was able to return to his part-time work at the Treasury Department. (He had recently been transferred there from the Attorney General's office.) In May his mother died. Her death was "the great dark cloud of my life—the only staggering, staying blow & trouble I have had—but *unspeakable*—my physical sickness, bad as it is, is nothing to it . . . "

In October, unable to work any longer. Walt moved to Camden, New Jersey, where his brother George lived with his wife, Louisa. He shared a sunny, south-facing third-floor

Interior of Whitman's home on
Mickle Street, Camden, New Jersey

apartment in the corner house at 322 Stevens Street. His health failed to improve, with one doctor after another giving him mistaken diagnoses. Not until 1878 did a neurologist tell him that his paralysis was caused by a ruptured blood vessel in the brain.

Camden was a small industrial and railroad city, across the river from Philadelphia. Walt had saved a good part of his postwar wages in Washington. With George and Louisa charging him a very low rent, and providing him with good food and companionship, this was comfortable living. He busied himself preparing the Centennial Edition of *Leaves*.

But while Walt had few worries, the nation plunged into deep despair. A depression that began in September 1873 soon became one of the biggest and worst. By 1877 it had engulfed nearly all but the rich. One out of five workers was jobless, and two out of five worked no more than half the year. That winter the count of unemployed stood at three million. Wages were cut as much as 50 percent, often to as little as one dollar a day. Public charities were besieged by sufferers. The streets swarmed with beggars. Hundreds of banks and businesses collapsed. Men, women, and children vanished from the factories. Miners climbed up out of the earth and left gaping holes empty for years to come. Farmers walked out of their fields and the plows rusted alone.

Walt saw on the streets homeless families whose look of "misery, terror and destitution" shocked him. What's wrong, he wrote, "is the social and economic organization, the treatment of working people by employers . . . If the United States, like the countries of the Old World, are also to grow vast crops of poor, desperate, dissatisfied, miserably-waged populations such as we see looming upon us of late years—steadily, even if slowly, eating into them like a cancer of lungs or stomach—then our republican experiment, notwithstanding all its surface successes, is at heart an unhealthy failure."

The poems Walt wrote during these troubled years reflect the changes he was going through. No longer did he praise industrial America; the anguish it was causing was almost too much to bear. In "Prayer of Columbus" he describes the great voyager as a seventy-year-old man ship-wrecked by poverty and neglect, "old, poor and paralyzed." Was he thinking of himself?

He seemed unable to deal directly with depression America. Instead, his poems avoid the reality of social evils and reach for the spiritual realm. He put the self, the body, and the nation behind him to create visions of the divine.

One of America's leading literary critics, Alfred Kazin, looking at the tall sweep of Walt's poetry, concluded that "the whole world . . . is open to Whitman's general loving-ness, which is boundless affirmation. Nothing may be excluded; nothing is higher or lower than anything else. He is the perfect democrat, in religion as in love and politics. There is no hierarchy in his determination to love every-thing and everyone in one full sweep."

Chapter 16

I'm Going Away

ALT LEFT CAMDEN OFTEN TO VISIT friends, give readings, attend the opera. On Tom Paine's 140th birthday he gave the memorial lecture in Philadelphia, and in 1879 began a long-running series of lectures on Lincoln. Although he despised his conventional poem, "O Captain!," he almost always recited it at the end of his Lincoln lectures. It was what the public wanted, so why not give it to them? In 1879, Walt took trains west to see the Great Plains and the Rockies. Visiting Burroughs on his place near the Hudson River, he rambled the countryside or strolled along the shore. He was often seen on the streets of Philadelphia carrying a basket filled with copies of *Leaves*, which he left at the door of those who ordered the book. Now the Camden Ferry across the Delaware provided the old pleasure of the Brooklyn Ferry, as he chatted with everyone aboard from pilots and deckhands to bootblacks and newsboys.

In the 1870s, Walt made a new friend, Richard Maurice Bucke, a noted therapist at a progressive mental clinic in Canada. Bucke loved *Leaves* and looked up Walt in Camden. He revered the poet as a prophet of man's divine potential, and in 1880 Walt visited the Bucke family in London, Ontario—his only trip outside the United States. He spent four months in Canada seeing much of the eastern part. Bucke wrote an idealized biography of Whitman, which he let Walt revise. Walt told him, "I am by no means the benevolent, equable, happy creature you portray—but let that pass—I have left it as you wrote."

For several years Walt spent parts of his summers at a farmhouse ten miles from Camden. It was the home of the

Whitman in the 1870s

Stafford family. Their eldest son, Harry, at eighteen was working in a Camden printshop when he met Walt in 1876. He became an affectionate "adopted" son to Walt, who often stayed for weeks at a time on the family farm. There he wrote parts of *Specimen Days* and prepared the 1881 edition of *Leaves*.

Walt took water-and-air baths daily in a nearby creek, hobbling barefooted in its muddy bottom, shouting lines from Shakespeare and singing old army songs. It was his gymnasium in nature and did much to improve his health.

He never gave up his passion for note-taking, and was always pausing to jot down what he saw and felt and thought. The notes, transformed, found their way into his poetry and prose.

Whatever Walt did, wherever he went, people recognized "the good gray poet." Nevertheless, he liked the image of the "solitary singer," and continued to promote it, complaining constantly that he was isolated and alone. Like most writers, he knew the sour taste of rejection slips and put-downs by critics. But most of the leading writers had long acknowledged his achievement. At home and abroad many called him America's greatest poet.

His work, both poetry and prose, appeared often in popular periodicals. He was not only successful as a magazine writer but was reprinted in several textbooks and anthologies. Always a promoter, he even wrote an anonymous article about himself for a New Jersey paper in 1876 that lamented that Walt Whitman had been totally ignored by his country. His poems, "still born" he said, met with "denial, disgust and scorn" from the literary establishment.

It was clever of Walt to plant the piece in that Republican paper, for it was a strong supporter of big business interests. If the *West Jersey Press* was sympathetic to Whitman,

A page from the notebooks Whitman kept,
recording everyday events—where he was,
what he did, whom he saw . . .

then upper class readers felt they should be, too. Their backing was expressed in gifts of money to the poet who had falsely portrayed himself as down on his luck.

The piece in the Jersey paper brought other poets to Walt's doorstep. Longfellow visited him that year, feeling greater regard for Walt now that Europeans had praised him highly. So, too, with Whittier and Lowell. And later on, in 1882, young Oscar Wilde, England's much praised poet and playwright, on a lecture tour of America, showed up in Camden to pay his respects to the older man. Much impressed, he returned a few months later: "There is no one in this wide great world of America," he said, "whom I love and honor so much."

It was the general public that was slow to recognize him and to read his poems. He must have felt envy when in 1877, on the seventieth birthday of Henry Wadsworth Longfellow, the poet was nationally celebrated, with schoolchildren everywhere honoring him. The whole world read Longfellow, the first American poet able to make a living from his writing. Not a poet of great originality (he was no Whitman!), yet beloved by all.

In the spring of 1884, Walt was able to buy his own house on Mickle Street in Camden. He was helped by cash gifts from people who believed the poet was almost destitute. A year later, others pitched in to buy him a horse and buggy.

Walt's closest companion in the last years of his life was Horace Traubel. Born in Camden in 1858, Traubel dropped out of school at twelve to work, like the young Walt, as a printer and reporter. When around twenty, Traubel got to know Walt and dropped by his home to sit with the poet and listen to his reminiscences. He began taking notes of almost everything Walt said, recording the talks as carefully as possible. Walt knew this, and didn't mind.

Traubel's socialist views sometimes led to quarrels with Walt. When the poet accepted a gift of $400 from Andrew Carnegie, Traubel was furious with him. What about the gross exploitation of the workers in Carnegie's steel mills, where thousands of people are never paid a living wage?

How can you accept charity from such a man? But Walt refused to criticize Carnegie. He accepted the steelmaster's unceasing attempt to portray himself as America's most liberal enlightened industrialist.

They quarreled, too, over Walt's poems praising the German Emperor Frederick Wilhelm I and Britain's Queen Victoria, rulers whose armies subjugated peoples of Asia and Africa for the profit of the business barons. Well, Walt would reply, they try to do right. Most of Walt's other friends were as shocked as young Traubel.

And then there was Walt's high regard for President Rutherford B. Hayes as "unifier" of the nation. Unifier? When his administration let the South crush Reconstruction with lynchings and bullets and plunge the black people into a hell of segregation?

As Walt's view of America grew more conservative, so did his poetic language. The idiom of the people, their pungent phrases, their salty tongue, their lively slang gave way to the "thee" and "thou" school. Now and then, however, you could hear eruptions of his buried 1850s writing, as when quoted in an 1892 press interview: "I should say we New Worlders are turning out the trickiest, slyest, cutest, most cheating people that ever lived."

During Walt's last four years, Traubel came to the feeble old man's bedside almost nightly to draw from him an oral history of his life. After the poet's death, he published three volumes of his record in *Walt Whitman in Camden*. Six more appeared later, edited by scholars after Traubel's death, the last of them in 1996.

Walt's final public appearance came in 1890 on the anniversary of Lincoln's death. In a wheelchair, pushed by a male nurse, he barely made it into the Philadelphia hall where 400 people, many of them society folk, were waiting

Walt's home on Mickle Street, Camden

for him. Sitting at a small table decorated with a spray of lilacs, he told of his first sight of Lincoln in New York on the way to his inauguration, of his observation of the President as he passed on the streets of Washington, and of Lincoln's murder in Ford's Theater, concluding with the usual recitation of "O Captain!" Safely home in Camden, he said to Traubel, "I came out of it alive!"

In 1889, Walt's seventieth birthday was celebrated by a large crowd gathered in a Camden hall. He was distressed

The poet, shortly before he died on March 26, 1892

when he learned the sponsors had not invited women. But some were invited after he objected. All along, hadn't women been his best readers? One feminist author had said he was "the only poet who had done justice to women."

> I am the poet of the woman the same as the man,
> And I say it is as great to be a woman as to be a man,
> And I say there is nothing greater than the mother of men.

Walt spoke little, just listened to the many speeches and messages honoring him, several from the foremost writers, such as Mark Twain. The literary feast was covered by the Philadelphia and New York press. The advance ticket sales paid for the wheelchair he had needed since suffering the strokes of the previous summer.

In January 1892, aware that his end was near, Walt made out his final will. He left most of his savings and his house to his retarded brother Ed. He chose Camden's Harleigh Cemetery as his burial site, and helped design a massive tomb that would hold not only himself but members of his family.

The poet lived long enough to complete a final edition of *Leaves of Grass*, published in 1892. He wanted it to be preferred to all previous ones. In his last poem he said good-bye to his creative powers: "I'm going away . . . I know not where/Or to what fortune, or whether I may ever see you again . . . "

In the late fall of 1891 he began to fail so rapidly that his doctors expected him to go in a few days. He defied them by lingering for three months more. Finally, suffering terribly, he caved in. On the evening of March 26, 1892, he died.

> I bequeath myself to the dirt to grow from the grass I love,
> If you want me again look for me under your boot-soles.
>
> You will hardly know who I am or what I mean.
> But I shall be good health to you nevertheless,
> And filter and fibre your blood.
>
> Failing to fetch me at first keep encouraged,
> Missing me one place search another,
> I stop somewhere waiting for you.
>
> —Closing lines from "Song of Myself"

Whitman's Camden, New Jersey, tomb,
which he designed himself

Chronology of Walt Whitman's Life

1819	Born May 31 at West Hills, near Huntington, Long Island, New York.
1823	Whitman family moves to Brooklyn.
1825–1830	Attends public school in Brooklyn.
1830	Office boy for doctor, lawyer.
1830–1834	Learns printing trade.
1835	Printer in New York City.
1836–1838	Returns to family on Long Island. First period of teaching.
1838–1839	Launches own newspaper, *Long Islander*, in Huntington.
1839–1841	Campaigns for Van Buren. Writes for *Long Island Democrat*. Returns to teaching on Long Island.
1840	Printer in Manhattan for weekly *New World*. Writes for *Democratic Review*.
1842–1848	Writes and edits for New York and Brooklyn papers. Publishes temperance novel, *Franklin Evans*.
1848	Goes south to edit *New Orleans Crescent*. After three months returns to Brooklyn. Edits Free Soil paper, the Brooklyn *Freeman*.
1849–1854	Runs printing shop and stationery store, does freelance journalism, builds and speculates in houses.

1855	Self-publishes *Leaves of Grass* in early July. Father dies July 11. Emerson writes to him July 21.
1856	Publishes second edition of *Leaves*. Visited at home by Alcott and Thoreau.
1857–1859	Edits Brooklyn *Daily Times*.
1860	Publishes third edition of *Leaves* in Boston.
1861	Civil War begins. Brother George Whitman enlists.
1862	In December travels to Virginia to locate brother George, reported wounded. Stays in camp two weeks. Moved by sight of battlefield wounded and dead, decides to relocate to Washington to help nurse war-wounded.
1863–1864	Works part-time in government office. Volunteers as male nurse in army hospitals. Begins friendship with O'Connors and their circle.
1864	On June 22 returns to Brooklyn because of illness.
1865	Lincoln assassinated. War ends. *Drum-Taps* printed, and sequel with "When Lilacs Last in the Dooryard Bloom'd."
1866–1867	Fourth edition of *Leaves* published. O'Connor publishes *Good Gray Poet*.
1867	First foreign edition of his poetry in England.
1870–1871	*Democratic Vistas* and fifth edition of *Leaves* published.
1873	First paralytic stroke January 23. Mother dies May 23. Moves in with brother George in Camden, New Jersey.
1874	Loses government job, his main source of income.
1876	Begins recuperative visits to Pennsylvania farm of Staffords. Sixth edition of *Leaves* published.

1877	Meets Canadian Dr. Richard M. Bucke, who becomes his adviser and biographer. Gives Tom Paine lecture in Philadelphia.
1878	Health improved, visits Manhattan, sees John Burroughs.
1879	Gives first Lincoln lecture, in New York. Travels west, stopping in St. Louis to visit with brother Jeff and family. Moves on to Colorado.
1880	Gives Lincoln lecture in Philadelphia, visits Dr. Bucke in Canada.
1881	Publishes seventh edition of *Leaves,* in Boston.
1882	Threatened with prosecution for obscenity by Boston authorities, publisher withdraws *Leaves.* Philadelphia publisher takes on book, and also publishes *Specimen Days.*
1883	Dr. Bucke publishes biography of Whitman, extensively edited by the poet.
1884	Buys house on Mickle Street, Camden.
1885–1887	Health worsening, gives some Lincoln lectures, but mostly stays at or near home.
1888	Horace Traubel, frequent visitor, begins taking notes of their conversations. Aided by Traubel, eighth edition of *Leaves* published. Suffers severe stroke in June.
1889	Seventieth birthday celebration held in Camden.
1891	*Goodbye My Fancy* printed, and ninth or "death-bed" edition of *Leaves* is published.
1892	Dies March 26, buried in Harleigh Cemetery, Camden.

For Further Reading

A great many editions of Whitman's poetry and prose have been published since his death in 1892. This list includes some suggestions of modern editions available in libraries or bookstores, plus some of the scholarly studies of Whitman I have used in my research. Those who wish to go beyond this list can check the much more detailed bibliography in *The Cambridge Companion to Walt Whitman*.

Modern Editions of Whitman's Writings

There are about a dozen modern editions of Whitman's writings. I found the most useful to be Norton's critical edition of *Leaves of Grass*, edited by Sculley Bradley and Harold W. Blodgett (New York: Norton, 1973). It contains not only all the poems through Whitman's last edition, but his prefaces, his prose statements on his role as artist, and a selection of criticism.

The other edition readily available is *The Portable Walt Whitman*, edited by Mark Van Doren (New York: Penguin, 1973). It contains 100 poems from *Leaves*, all of the prose works from *Democratic Vistas* and *Specimen Days*, plus a chronology and bibliographical checklist. Both of these are available in paperback.

Works About Walt Whitman

Allen, Gay Wilson. *The Solitary Singer*, rev. ed. Chicago: University of Chicago Press, 1985.

Allen, Gay Wilson and Ed Filsom, eds. *Walt Whitman and the World*. Ames: University of Iowa Press, 1995.

Bloom, Harold, ed. *Walt Whitman: Modern Critical Views*. New York: Chelsea House, 1985.

Brooks, Van Wyck. *The Times of Melville and Whitman*. New York: Dutton, 1947.

Erkilla, Betsy. *Whitman: The Political Poet*. New York: Oxford, 1989.

Greenspan, Ezra, ed. *The Cambridge Companion to Walt Whitman*. New York: Cambridge, 1995.

Kreig, Joann P. *Whitman and the Irish*. Iowa City: University of Iowa Press, 2000.

Loving, Jerome. *Walt Whitman: The Song of Himself*. Berkeley: University of California, 1999.

Morris, Roy K. Jr. *The Better Angel: Walt Whitman in the Civil War*. New York: Oxford, 2000.

Myerson, Joel. *Whitman in His Own Time*. Iowa City: University of Iowa, 2000.

Padgett, Ron, ed. *The Teachers and Writers Guide to Walt Whitman*. New York: Teachers & Writers Collaborative, 1991.

Perlman, Jim, and Dan Campion, eds. *Walt Whitman: The Measure of His Song*. Duluth: Holy Cow Press, 1998.

Reynolds, David S. *Walt Whitman's America: A Cultural Biography*. New York: Vintage, 1996.

Widner, Edward L. *Young America: The Flowering of Democracy in New York City*. New York: Oxford, 1999.

Wiener, Gary, ed. *Readings on Walt Whitman*. San Diego: Greenhaven Press, 1999.

Ziff, Larzer. *Literary Democracy*. New York: Penguin, 1982.

For those who wish to keep abreast of new material on Whitman there is *The Whitman Quarterly Review*, containing articles, book reviews, and bibliographical updates. Its address is 308 EPB, the University of Iowa, Iowa City, IA 52242.

Films, videos, and audio recordings have been produced on various aspects of Whitman's life and work.

For those who have access to the Internet, searching for Walt Whitman with any good search engine will lead to many sites. Please remember that all sites are sources needing to be checked, evaluated, and compared with other sources.

Visiting Walt Whitman Sites

Walt Whitman House, an 1810 farmhouse, where he spent the first four years of his life, is now a museum. Open all year: Wed-Fri 1–4, Sat and Sun 10–4. Closed holidays. Free admission. School and group tours by appointment.

Walt Whitman House, 246 Old Walt Whitman Rd., Huntington Station, N.Y. 11748, tel. (631) 427-5240.

Walt Whitman House at 330 Mickle Street, Camden, N.J., where he spent the last eight years of his life. For information on visits to the house, which is overseen by the State of New Jersey, call (609) 964-5383 or (609) 726-1191.

Walt Whitman Association, at 326 Mickle Street, has a library with original manuscripts, letters, first editions, and photos of Whitman. Visits by appointment. Contact Walt Whitman Association at P.O. Box 1493, Camden N.J. 08101. Or call (609) 963-0122.

Web Sites on Walt Whitman

http://jefferson.village.virginia.edu/whitman/
See digitized images of Whitman's works in their original form.

http://www.everypoet.com/archive/poetry/Walt_Whitman/walt_whitman_contents.htm
Whitman's complete Leaves of Grass.

http://www.liglobal.com/walt/
Information and links on the poet.

http://www.poets.org/poets/poets.cfm?prmID = 127&CFID = 2575954&CFTOKEN = 86354348
A biography and links to his works.

http://www.cyberenet.net/ ~ kelta/whitman.html
Material about Whitman's birthplace in Camden, New Jersey

http://college.hmco.com/english/heath/syllabuild/iguide/whitman.html
Analysis of some of Whitman's work particularly valuable for teachers and students in studying his poetry.

Index

Page numbers in *italics* refer to illustrations.

Cover photograph courtesy of Library of Congress

Photographs courtesy of Library of Congress (Charles E. Feinberg/Walt Whitman Collection): pp. 2, 11, 18 (both), 135, 141, 146, 149; Museum of the City of New York: pp. 22 (*Winter Scene in Brooklyn, New York, 1817-20.* Oil on canvas, Louisa A. Coleman, 53.2), 23 (*View of Manhattan from Brooklyn Heights/The Hill Bennett-Clover View from Brooklyn Heights*, 1837, 29.100.2354); Culver Pictures, Inc.: p. 26; New York Historical Society: p. 31; The Smithtown Library: p. 34; The Granger Collection, New York: pp. 41, 44, 65, 120; University of Virginia Library/The Albert H. Small Special Collections Library: pp. 47 (from *Franklin Evans*), 114 (Walt Whitman Collection #3829-H. Clifton Waller Barrett Library); Bahley-Whitman Collection, Ohio Wesleyan University: pp. 68, 147; New York Public Library Picture Collection: p. 73; Library of Congress: pp. 94, 99, 102, 104, 143; Duke University: p. 96 (Rare Book, Manuscript & Special Collections Library)

About the Author

To his biographies of the poets Langston Hughes and Carl Sandburg, Milton Meltzer now adds the life of Walt Whitman. He has written over one hundred books for young people and adults in the fields of history, biography, and social issues, and has written and edited for newspapers, magazines, radio, television, and films.

Five of his books have been finalists for the National Book Award. He has won the Regina Medal, Christopher, Jane Addams, Carter G. Woodson, Jefferson Cup, Washington Book build, Olive Branch, and Golden Kite awards. In 2001, he was the recipient of the American Library Association's Laura Ingalls Wilder Award, honoring his lifetime body of work. Many of his books have been chosen for the honor lists of the American Library Association, the National Council of Teachers of English, the National Council for the Social Studies, the New York Public Library's annual Books for the Teen Age, and the *New York Times* Best Books of the Year list.

Born in Worcester, Massachusetts, Mr. Meltzer was educated at Columbia University. He lives with his wife in New York City. They have two daughters and two grandsons.